# ADMITTED ASSASSIN

## ROSCOE WHITE AND THE MURDER OF PRESIDENT KENNEDY

**PENIEL UNLIMITED, LLC**
Michael and Kelly Marcades, Publishers
326 Valley Star Drive
Canyon Lake, Texas 78133
http://www.penielunlimited.com

The vision of PENIEL UNLIMITED, LLC, Dr. Michael Glenn Marcades founding President, is to provide superior services related to publishing manuscripts worthy of public access. Since its inception, PENIEL UNLIMITED, LLC has taken particular interest in manuscripts associated with, but not limited to, the assassination of President John F. Kennedy, choral music pedagogy, children's books, and more. PENIEL UNLIMITED, LLC . . . the "author's choice."



Printed in the United States of America



ISBN: 979-8-218-34604-1

This book may be purchased for varied educational purposes. For information, contact michaelmarcades@gmail.com or www.penielunlimited.com.



Special appreciation to Mary Ann Moorman (Krahmer) for granting permission to utilize her photograph.

Book Cover Design & Production by Daniel Whisnant
(www.suissemade.com)
10 9 8 7 6 5 4 3 2

# ADMITTED ASSASSIN

## ROSCOE WHITE AND THE MURDER OF PRESIDENT KENNEDY

**By Ricky White**
**as told to**
**J. Gary Shaw and Brian K. Edwards**

**Published 2023 PENIEL UNLIMITED, LLC**

# CONTENTS

# ACKNOWLEDGMENTS

First and foremost, we are so grateful to our long-suffering wives, Karen and Christy. Their encouragement, assistance, and sacrifice in dealing with us during the long and arduous process of writing this daunting story are greatly appreciated.

Completion of this project would have never happened without the cooperation and encouragement of Ricky and Tricia White. From the beginning, it was apparent that our telling of this deeply complex story without supporting documentation, first-hand accounts, and photographs would be impossible. Ricky and Tricia allowed the authors unlimited access to family photos, private correspondence, medical records, and personal interviews – all of which provided vital insight into the complete story of Ricky's father. Most of the photos herein have been seen only by members of the White family. For such access, the authors are grateful and honored.

Until shortly before she died in 1991, Geneva, Roscoe White's wife, gave the authors a glimpse into her life with her husband through numerous audio recordings from the 1970s. Her contribution was indispensable to this work.

Furthermore, we thank posthumously Bud Fensterwald, Larry Ray Harris, and Larry Howard. These pioneers of the JFK assassination research community were the first to investigate the Roscoe White story. Their considerable contributions will not be forgotten.

A great big thank you to our editors and publishers, Kelly and Michael Marcades. They went above and beyond for us. As many know, Michael is the son of Melba Youngblood Marcades, aka, "Rose Cherami." His book about his mother's life, *ROSE CHERAMI: Gathering Fallen Petals,* is about her life — and her intriguing link to Jack Ruby and the JFK assassination.

And finally, in no particular order, we recognize the following individuals for their contributions and support in helping us tell this story: Robert Groden, William Klaber, Casey Quinlan, Leslie Sharp, Chris Gallop, David Knight, Lt. Colonel David McElreath, USMC (ret.), Bill Kelly, Sara Peterson, Katana Zachry, Dan Storper, and Joe West (posthumously).

,

# COINCIDENTAL?

Photo captions - clockwise:

The admitted assassin, **Roscoe A. White**, U.S. Marine – Expert Marksman, ca.1960....

The admitted assassin's wife, **Geneva**, poses – and goes to work for – Roscoe's friend, **Jack Ruby**, in September 1963....

The admitted assassin, **Roscoe White**, goes to work for the Dallas Police Department on October 7, 1963....

The **"Patsy"** – **Lee Harvey Oswald**, Roscoe's and Ruby's friend, goes to work at the Texas School Book Depository, in Dallas on October 18, 1963.

# PREFACE:
## J. Gary Shaw and Brian K. Edwards

As Oliver Stone noted in his controversial film, *JFK*, the assassination of President John F. Kennedy "*. . . was probably one of the most terrible moments in the history of our country.*"

A criminal investigation of this importance and magnitude should never have to be questioned. It's unfortunate for the American people that the Dallas Police, the FBI, the Central Intelligence Agency, and the United States government failed to bring the true killers of the President to justice. After six decades, many questions remain unanswered. The documented and demonstrable cover-up by each of these groups is by its very nature a conspiracy. And each participant in this conspiracy, minor or major, could be considered an accessory after the fact.

Today, as we write, many important facts related to the assassination of President Kennedy remain hidden from the public. Thousands of pages remain classified and may never be made available. In an open society, how do we allow this to occur? Without access to the facts, there can only be speculation and theories about how and why the President was killed. Hiding the truth from the American people engenders mistrust, suspicion, and contempt of our democratic systems of government. No longer can we rely on our politicians, corrupt government agencies, and powerbrokers to decide what is in our best interest. Obviously, it's *their* best interest that matters.

As free citizens, we are entitled to know the truth about the events of November 22, 1963. Knowing the truth may deeply affect those who have chosen to remain uninformed and rely on the mass media for their daily dose of reality. But at the end of the day, we have the right, the need, and the desire to know more.

This book is an account of a concerted effort by Ricky White and others to either verify or challenge certain evidence and information implicating his father in the ambush that killed President Kennedy in Dallas, Texas.

This story is **not** just another theory; rather, it is an account of the quest for truth by an honest and sincere man who believes his father was directly involved in the plot to kill President Kennedy.

The man is Ricky Don White, son of Roscoe Anthony White. From what we have learned through resolute research, Ricky's suspicions about his father's involvement in the assassination appear to be justified.

This story details the connections between Roscoe Anthony White, a man who secreted away information that linked him directly to what has been called the crime of the century. There are too many connections to be dismissed as mere coincidence. Ricky's father purposely left behind this material that points to a strong relationship between himself and certain forces behind the murder of President Kennedy.

Roscoe Anthony "Rock" White, like the alleged assassin Lee Harvey Oswald, was a former United States Marine. White joined the Dallas Police Department six weeks prior to President Kennedy's arrival in Dallas. At the same time, Oswald began his employment at the Texas School Book Depository.

While in the Marines, both soldiers were stationed together at some of the same Far East military bases. Many researchers believe that Oswald was recruited into covert intelligence work while on active duty at this time. The same could hold true for Roscoe White who appears to have been an ideal candidate for similar recruitment.

Interestingly, perhaps suspiciously, in September 1963, eight weeks before the assassination, Roscoe's wife, Geneva, began working for Jack Ruby. Two photographs confirm this; one of which was published in *TIME* magazine. Ruby would later murder the accused assassin, Oswald, in the basement of Dallas police headquarters.

Evidence also indicates that before Roscoe joined the Dallas Police Department, he and another officer, J.D. Tippit, were acquainted with each other. Forty-five minutes after Kennedy was shot in Dealey Plaza, Officer Tippit was shot and killed – allegedly by Lee Oswald.

The circumstances surrounding the shooting of Tippit, an ex-Army paratrooper, remain shrouded in mystery even to this day. Major discrepancies in the evidence of his murder have never been adequately explained by the police, the FBI, the Warren Commission, or the House Select Committee on Assassinations.

From his position within the police department, Roscoe would have had the perfect cover to monitor events before, during, and after the assassination. He could have known the time and precise route of the presidential motorcade as well as the logistics for Lee Oswald's transfer to the county jail. In addition, Roscoe could have had access to the progress of both murder investigations, who the witnesses were, and what they were saying.

In 1971, as he lay dying in Parkland Hospital from severe burns suffered in an industrial explosion and fire, White confessed to his minister, Reverend Jack Shaw, that he had sinned against his country and *"...had taken lives on domestic and foreign soil."* Before he succumbed to his injuries, he also told his minister that the explosion and fire was not an accident but was perpetrated by a man he knew. During another prayer and counseling session with his pastor, White admitted that he had led a "double life" which began while he was in the Marines.

Is this just more fodder for another JFK conspiracy theory provided by conspiracy theorists? The authors do not believe it is. Although the story will likely continue to be dismissed by many, it remains a complicated and compelling story. Also, the information and evidence obtained from Ricky White persuasively substantiates it.

There remains a remote possibility that this evidence may have been prepared and planted to further confuse or discredit independent research into the assassination. **The authors do not believe this is so!**

The existing evidence strongly suggests that Roscoe White himself carefully preserved this self-incriminating evidence, believing it would one day be discovered and disclosed.

Furthermore, it is the author's firm belief that as an assassin, Roscoe White is an appreciably better candidate than the accused Lee Harvey Oswald. The following is a quick comparison of the two men's bona fides:

– Lee's marksmanship rating in the Marines was mediocre to poor while Roscoe's was expert.

– Lee, rather than take credit for killing the President and Officer Tippit, loudly and aggressively denied any involvement in either crime.

– Roscoe took great pains to leave behind clues, evidence, and a hand-written statement confirming his role in the shootings.

– Lee's Russian wife, Marina, has strongly denied publicly that her husband killed the President.

– Roscoe's wife, Geneva, worked at the Carousel Club and overheard plans to kill the President being discussed by her husband and Jack Ruby.

– Lee acquired employment with the Texas School Book Depository about five weeks before the assassination.

– Roscoe obtained employment with the Dallas Police Department about six weeks before the assassination, allowing him the perfect cover and freedom to move about the assassination site and police headquarters.

It's no secret that Jesse Curry, Dallas's Police Chief at the time of the assassination, admitted publicly:

> *"We don't have any proof that Oswald fired the rifle, and never did. Nobody's yet been able to put him in that building with a gun in his hand" (Dallas Morning News, 11/6/69).*

Because of his deep love for his country and at enormous personal risk and even embarrassment, Ricky Don White's desire is to fulfill what he believes to have been his father's intention — namely, to reveal what he knew about that fateful day.

Ricky's story about his father's involvement in the Kennedy assassination has often been described by cynics and critics as: erroneous, fabricated, disinformation, misinformation, controversial, and an elaborate hoax. Even so, the authors believe that the Roscoe White story has merit warranting consideration for further serious research and study.

And, as Ricky himself wrote: *"...do not believe anything you've read or heard about this story until you read this book."* His co-authors strongly agree. Those who have attempted to denigrate and detract from the story have done so with insufficient and/or faulty knowledge. This work presents material that has not been seen or previously made available but to a few people other than the authors.

Many ***think*** they know about Roscoe White — but few actually ***know*** the full Roscoe White story.

Much has been written and opined regarding Roscoe White and we will neither attempt to refute nor accept these various assessments, assumptions, and conclusions. Our sole intent is to place this material before the reader for their own information and study. In so doing, perhaps they can assist the authors in better understanding this multifaceted and complex story.

The result of the authors' extensive research and study has led to our unwavering confidence that the contrived evidence of Oswald's guilt is far outweighed by the convincing evidence found in the Roscoe White story.

This particular journey represents only a portion of our personal quest for truth — for President John Kennedy, for Lee Oswald… *and* for Roscoe White.

Please understand that this book takes a hardline approach to the malfeasance and dereliction of duty on the part of some of the governmental agents involved in the investigation of the Roscoe White story. While we often cite these agencies as a whole, it is not our intent, nor our desire, to demean or disparage the many honest and dutiful federal agents and employees who faithfully serve our nation day in and day out.

On the other hand, to those of these agencies who try to use the excuse: *"We were just following orders,"* we suggest they remember those so-called "good soldiers" who tried to utilize this same lame excuse regarding the atrocities of World War II.

# FOREWORD I:
## by Ricky Don White

**With his explicit approval, this Foreword represents and presents the words, thoughts, and wishes of Ricky Don White. It is an edited version of what he has written and verbalized to his co-authors, J. Gary Shaw and Brian K. Edwards.**

My name is Ricky Don White, and I was born November 24, 1960. On November 24, 1963, I was celebrating my third birthday when Jack Ruby shot Lee Harvey Oswald in the basement of the Dallas police station. On that day, my father, Roscoe Anthony White, was an officer with the Dallas Police Department.

In 1971, when I was eleven years old, my father was killed in a suspicious accident at his workplace.

In the spring of 1978, *[As the House Select Committee on Assassinations was winding down its investigation – the Authors]* a family friend told me the federal government was going to name my father as one of the killers of President Kennedy.

Four years later in 1982, I rediscovered my father's Marine Corps footlocker. One of the first items that caught my eye was a green zippered bank bag from Wynnewood State Bank that contained two small keys. Not knowing the significance of the keys, I put the bag aside and looked through the rest of my father's collection.

Another item in the footlocker was my father's personal diary. In one of the entries, he mentioned a large sum of money in a safe deposit box but did not identify the name of the bank. I naturally assumed one of the keys would unlock at least one safe deposit box at the Wynnewood State Bank in Dallas.

In the beginning, my only thought was to find the safe deposit box and recover the money my father had secreted away for our family. At the time, seeking publicity about my family was the furthest thing from my mind. These discussions only came about after I began sharing my father's story with others.

Sometime later, as I continued my slow and laborious reading of the diary, I came across the most heartbreaking and devastating admission any son could ever experience. There, written in my father's own hand, he admitted his direct role in the assassination of President Kennedy. (Note: As the reader will later learn, the diary was stolen from my home by an agent of the Federal Bureau of Investigation.).

In May 1990, I met J. Gary Shaw for the first time at the JFK Assassination Information Center (JFKAIC) in Dallas. I had been told that he was a leading expert on the Kennedy assassination. I explained to Gary what I had found, hoping he could provide some guidance on what to do with the material. Gary listened attentively and was genuinely interested in the story. We quickly became good friends.

Soon I began sharing my father's story with Larry Ray Harris, Larry Howard, J. Gary Shaw and Washington-based attorney Bud Fensterwald during my many visits to the JFK Assassination Information Center (JFKAIC).

In June 1990, following a clue from my father's diary, I searched the attic of my grandparents' home and found a steel canister hidden in the rafters. Inside the canister was a small green scrapbook, my father's Marine Corps dog tag, and three typed messages encased in clear laminate. These messages were addressed to "Mandarin", a codename used by my father in describing his role in the President's assassination. Included in the heading portion of the messages was my father's military serial number. These were extra pieces of a puzzle no one else had and I was unsure what my next step should be.

Gary Shaw eventually contacted journalist Earl Golz, a noted investigative reporter and JFK assassination expert to write a story about these latest discoveries. On August 5, 1990, Golz's story appeared on the front page of the *Austin American-Statesman* newspaper. The following day, the JFKAIC held a press conference where I told the world about my father's confessed involvement in the Kennedy assassination.

In 2018, Gary introduced me to Brian Edwards, a former police officer and educator. Gary said that Brian is well-respected in the assassination community and has a reputation as being a meticulous and thorough researcher. Gary assured me Brian would be an asset to the project.

Brian and Gary have labored to produce the most definitive account of my father's life and his connection to one of the darkest days in our history. In telling my story, Gary and Brian's dedication to the truth has provided my family with the knowledge this story has been told as accurately and honestly as possible.

Many of the revelations found in this book are not mine; rather, they are the results of many hours of investigative work on the part of many researchers too numerous to mention here, but some are identified in the “Acknowledgments" section of this book.

For me, this work is a personal narrative of the father I barely knew, who loved me, his family, and his country. This is also about my journey of the last forty-plus years of wanting the truth to be known about my father, Roscoe Anthony White. I am obligated to tell his story because of the clues he left behind.

Don’t believe anything you’ve read or heard about this story until you read this book. Those who attempt to undermine this story do so without knowing the truth. Much of the material contained in this book has never been seen outside the White family. My sincere thanks to Gary and Brian for taking on this project and telling my father’s story to the world; a story I *know* he wanted told.

This story has been dismissed by the FBI, the media, high-government officials, and many in the assassination research community. It is my hope this will help put an end to the misinformation, disinformation, and outright obfuscation regarding my father and the cryptic clues he left behind.

After reviewing all the information and evidence, YOU be the judge as to its validity.

Ricky Don White, 2023.

# FOREWORD II:
## A Word from J. Gary Shaw

It's been 33 years since I was first introduced to the Roscoe White story by Roscoe's son, Ricky Don White. I believed the story then — I believe it now.

In retrospect, many of the decisions and actions taken in 1990 by me and my two JFK Assassination Information Center (JFKAIC) partners were premature and, in some cases, just plain wrong.

In my opinion, we were premature in inviting an investigative reporter into our circle to write a news story about Ricky Don White and his discovery of information and evidence of his father's admission of his involvement in the assassination of President John F. Kennedy and other events of November 22-24, 1963. I believe we were just plain wrong in calling for a major news conference and announcing to the world that we had hard evidence of a confession from one of the President's assassins.

I strongly opposed both decisions but was outvoted by my JFKAIC partners, Bud Fensterwald and Larry Howard. My opposition was simply based on my belief that the entire story required much more research, investigation, and verification. However, in retrospect, I must admit that my opposition was somewhat tempered by a thought-provoking handwritten letter sent to me and Larry Howard by Bud Fensterwald. He wrote:

*July 20, 1990*

*Dear Gary and Larry,*

*Just for the record I wish to state that, in my view, delay until August 20th is very unwise & very dangerous. Delay can result in one or more deaths, and may screw up the whole detail to boot.*

*You might remind Ricky that I fully intend to hold a press conference in Washington on Aug 2, whether he goes forward in Dallas the day before. Tell him nicely but tell him.*

*Your nervous friend,*
*Bud*

Maybe my partners were right; a speedy and widespread release of the information might have been best . . . and safest.

However, the lack of adequate research and investigation resulted in some ill-advised and false statements made by all involved, including Ricky. We misspoke and perhaps overstated our case, but these comments certainly were neither purposely made nor intentionally deceitful. And, some of our statements were simply misunderstood, misinterpreted, and overblown by the media and others.

In retrospect, the news conference was harmful and gave rise to much of the distrust and outright dismissal of Ricky White and his "bombshell" story. The almost frantic and negative response to the story by many in the JFK research community, mainstream media, and government agencies seemed to validate my position to take a slower and more cautious approach.

Numerous people have claimed that this story has been "debunked." The word "debunked" basically means: *"to show that something (such as a belief or theory) is not true; to show the falseness of (a story, idea, statement, etc.).* Truth is, simply proclaiming something or someone has been "debunked" is neither proof nor evidence. Much of the time, it's only someone's hyped-up, overblown opinion. And — the full Roscoe White story "debunks" the "debunker."

By 1996, I had packed away my Roscoe White files. Looking back at those early days, JFK assassination research and investigation was a tedious, time-consuming, and expensive process. Research tools like the Internet, *Google, Ancestry.com*, cellular communication, and the very essential Mary Ferrell Foundation did not exist. Today, these essential tools have been put to good use in writing *ADMITTED ASSASSIN.*

In 2017, while attending the JFK Lancer conference in Dallas, I sat in on a presentation about eyewitness Ed Hoffman. The presenter was Brian Edwards, a former police officer and college educator. Brian's research of the Hoffman story was extremely well-documented and professionally presented. Brian and I had met on previous occasions but had never personally interacted.

I liked him, — and I liked his straightforward approach to the case. And, since I was finally writing about what I knew and believed about the Roscoe White story, I decided to ask

Brian if he would be interested in being my co-author. Brian quickly agreed to help.

Brian told me he had been interested in the story since 1990 after he attended a private viewing of a film by JFK Assassination Information Center Co-Director Larry Howard. In that film, he saw some of the early research the Center had done on the subject. He believed the story had merit and thought that using a police officer as an assassin made perfect sense.

While writing this book, I allowed Brian unlimited access to my private, extensive research files and documents relating to Roscoe White. Even then, certain areas of Roscoe White's life, such as his time with the Dallas Police Department, are unknown. We know that Roscoe was hired on October 7, 1963, and attended the police academy from December 4, 1963, until February 28, 1964.

However, his activities between October 7 and December 4, 1963, are unknown. Oddly, nothing in his personnel file indicates where he worked after graduation from the academy; his file is void of any evaluations, commendations, awards, or citizen complaints.

On the other hand, on page one of the HSCA's final report, investigators Blackmer and Walsh wrote:

> *"Mrs. Geneva Dees, formally Mrs. Roscoe White of Dallas was interviewed concerning facts about her late husband who at the time of the assassination of Pres. Kennedy and the subsequent Dallas Police Investigation of the assassination*

> *was the police photographer and "film processor" for the homocide [sic] division . . . "*

It is unclear how or where these investigators obtained this information about Roscoe's duties while in the Dallas Police Department. Currently, there are no documents in his personnel file indicating where he was assigned after graduating from the police academy on February 28, 1964.

Some researchers have written that Roscoe was assigned to the crime scene search team as a photographer, while others believe he worked in the Robbery/Homicide Unit. Andy Burke, Ricky's friend, interviewed former Dallas police officer Bill Anglin, who knew and worked with Roscoe. Anglin told Burke, *"Roscoe was on a special enforcement unit in the patrol division. That unit dealt with riots, sniper . . . it was a tactical unit."* Through interviews with Ricky and other members of the White family, it became apparent that no one could explain, with any degree of certainty, what Roscoe's role was while employed with the police department.

This book is our best effort to "show and tell" the complete Roscoe White story — just as it was passed down by the man who admitted his role in the killing of President John F. Kennedy.

On more than one occasion, Ricky, in so many words, confessed to me his heartfelt feelings concerning divulging his father's admitted participation in the Kennedy assassination. Ricky further said that it was apparent that his father became deeply remorseful regarding his involvement in the murder of President Kennedy. Undoubtedly, that remorse led Roscoe to leave behind carefully preserved clues and artifacts regarding that ghastly event. Moreover, Ricky also told me that he believed his father intended for him to discover this material and tell the story. For this reason – even though it saddened and embarrassed him and his family to do so – Ricky wholeheartedly believed that <u>he was obligated to tell the full Roscoe White story</u>.

***"The true strength of rulers and emotions lies not in the armies or emotions, but in the belief of men that they are inflexibly open and truthful and legal. As soon as a government departs from that standard, it ceases to be anything more than 'the gang in possession' and its days are numbered."***

***— H. G. Wells***

# PROLOGUE:

## The "DEEP STATE" Initiative

## J. Gary Shaw

This book tells the story of a self-confessed assassin; a soldier employed by a secret organization dedicated to operating under its own dictatorial rules and guidelines. His confession was found in writings and artifacts he had hidden away before his sudden and tragic death in 1971. His once well-camouflaged "employer," now dubbed by many as "the deep state," has slowly been exposed and acknowledged by thinking Americans.

The term ***"DEEP STATE"*** has been defined as ***"A type of government made up of potentially secret and unauthorized networks of power operating independently of the State's political leadership in pursuit of their own agenda and goals."*** In other words, a government made up of individuals who believe that they — and they alone — are of sufficient intellect and ability to rule and reign over the masses. All others are not only unqualified to do so, they need only to be attended to, not listened to.

On the left is Major Carlton S. Coon (1904-1981), an American anthropologist and past president of the American Association of Physical Anthropologists.

On the right is General William J. "Wild Bill" Donovan, head of the Office of Strategic Services (OSS) in WWII — and founding father of the Central Intelligence Agency (CIA).

Please read slowly and carefully about some of the prime originators of this deep state mentality, followed by their descriptions of this pompous deep state rationale.

Major Coon's theories on race were widely disputed during his life and are considered pseudoscientific in the field of modern anthropology. His views on racial superiority were aligned with white supremacy.

In 1943, at the height of WWII, Coon wrote a letter to General Donovan advocating that American intelligence agencies adopt a policy of assassination and form an ultra-elite and secret assassination council. Coon wrote:

> *"The world is now too small and too tight to permit continuation of the process of trial and error... Therefore,* ***some other power, some third class of individuals, aside from*** [i.e., superior] ***the leaders and scholars*** *must exist, and this third-class must have the task of thwarting mistakes, diagnosing areas of political world disequilibrium and nipping the causes of potential disturbances in the bud...* [Therefore] ***There must be a body of men whose task it is to throw out the rotten apples*** [i.e., dispose of — assassinate] ***as soon as the first spots of decay appear. A body of this nature must exist undercover*** [i.e., in secret]**. *It must either be a power unto itself or be given the broadest discretionary powers by the highest human* authorities."** [i.e., secret government, the deep state] (edited for length and emphasis added).

The obvious questions that arise from such a chilling proposal are: (1) Who elects, or appoints, this higher power *"third class of individuals?"* And (2) who elects, or appoints, these *"highest human authorities"* who can mandate the *"broadest discretionary powers"* to this *"third class of individuals?"*

Eleven years later, in 1954, President Eisenhower appointed a panel of consultants to conduct a study of the covert activities of the Central Intelligence Agency. Lt. Gen. James H. "Jimmy" Doolittle was appointed the committee's chairman. The study is commonly called "The Doolittle Report," a 69-page report that remained classified for many years. The following statement was one of the major recommendations of this report:

> *"Hitherto acceptable norms of human conduct do not apply. If the United States is to survive, long-standing American concepts of 'fair play' must be reconsidered. We must develop effective espionage and counterespionage services and must learn to subvert, sabotage and destroy our enemies by more clever, more sophisticated and more effective methods than those used against us. It may become necessary that the American people be made acquainted with, understand and support this fundamentally repugnant philosophy."*

William D. Pawley, one of the four committee members, was a close friend of CIA Director Allen Dulles. Dulles played a significant role in the CIA's policy of "Executive Action" — a plan to remove unfriendly foreign leaders from power.

Just five months before the assassination, Pawley participated in and helped finance a clandestine CIA action involving Cuba called Operation Tilt.

Perhaps coincidentally, General Doolittle was a very close friend of David H. Byrd. In 1963, Byrd owned the infamous

Texas School Book Depository in Dallas. In Byrd's obituary, Doolittle calls him *"a substantial friend of mine."*

**Disclaimer: This book is NOT about the Donovan's or Coon's of the world. It IS, however, the story of a man who "filled the bill" of an assassin in a secret assassination program such as the one proposed by Coon. Government documents have revealed that an elite and secret apparatus DID exist and was operational in 1963. This book IS about Roscoe A. "Rock" White, a man who confessed his role as an assassin for just such a secret assassination program. The confession, writings, and artifacts he left behind can only be construed as his sincere desire to reveal some of the facts surrounding the President's murder.**

And, for the record, it is this author's firm belief that the solution to the perplexing and exasperating question as to who ordered and carried out the assassination of President Kennedy will never be found in any government documents. *If* such documentation *ever* existed within this government's files and/or archives, they were undoubtedly destroyed long ago.

At present, anyone with reasonable intelligence who examines the extant evidence without bias and preconceived ideas will be forced to conclude that the President was murdered by a criminal conspiracy and none of the conspirators have ever been identified or brought to justice.

Those who came to the insanely absurd conclusion that two lone nuts — and *only* two lone nuts — perpetrated the assassinations on that November weekend in Dallas must have had a learning disability, or they were personally involved in the crime, or they were/are part of its deep-state-led cover-up. They should be dismissed and ignored completely; and to argue with such a mindset is, and always will be, an exercise in futility and frustration.

**That Lee Harvey Oswald did not kill anyone is unquestionably a proven fact, and our goal now should be – to find out who did.**

That an ultra-secret organization took it upon themselves to decide that President Kennedy had to be removed from office is clear. In their minds, President Kennedy had shown himself to be a threat to worldwide peace, and more importantly, a peril to the bottom line of the "military-industrial complex" about which former President Eisenhower had warned the American people. His warning was not new.

Following World War I, President Woodrow Wilson recognized this and made the following statement:

[We are] *"...no longer a Government by conviction and the vote of the majority, but a Government by the opinion, and duress of a small group of dominant men."*

*"...there is a power somewhere so organized, so subtle, so watchful, so interlocked, so complete, so pervasive, that they*

*had better not speak above their breath when they speak in condemnation of it."*

Continuing in this vein, New Orleans District Attorney Jim Garrison wrote in his book, *Heritage of Stone*, the most accurate description of this nation's ongoing dilemma:

> *"Until the work of the Kennedy assassins is undone, presidents will come and go but the warfare machine and its extensive intelligence tentacles, domestic, as well as foreign, will remain in control. The assassination [of John F Kennedy] reduced the President of the United States to a transient official, a servant of the warfare conglomerate [the "Deep State"]. His assignment is to speak as often as possible about the nation's desire for peace, while he serves as a business agent with Congress for the military and their hardware manufacturers."*

Roscoe White knew for whom he worked and who was paying for his services. He knew what was expected of him and trusted those above him. He was familiar with their methods and how he received his orders; what to do with those orders. Instead of destroying the orders for him to kill *"a threat to worldwide peace"* (President Kennedy), he chose to hide them away hoping one day they would be found. His reason for not destroying these orders will probably never be fully understood. Perhaps he felt it was his only way to protect his family — and hopefully himself.

According to his minister, Roscoe became remorseful for his past deeds and wanted to leave that life behind. After making his intentions known to his confederates, he was no longer deemed an asset, but a liability — a liability that probably got him killed. His carefully preserved "protection" was left behind and later found by his son, Ricky.

This book is about Ricky White's discovery of his father's carefully preserved and hidden-away materials and the intriguing story of his attempt to follow his father's desire and disclose the compelling information about the death of the president.

# CHAPTER ONE:
## The Tragic and Convenient Death of Roscoe White

*Note to the Reader: This opening chapter is written in narrative nonfiction form. The dialogue presented is an accurate portrayal of the people, events and emotions surrounding the tragic and untimely death of Roscoe White. The information and descriptions herein are derived from countless interviews with family, friends, acquaintances, witnesses and documents. This is the only section of the book that uses this format. — The Authors.*

Thursday, September 23, 1971, began like any other fall day in Dallas, Texas. Two employees of the M & M Equipment and Rental Company at 10625 Ferguson Road had just returned to their workshop from a late afternoon coffee break at a local diner. Their plans were to work extra hours to complete repairs on an industrial forklift.

*10625 Ferguson Road, Dallas, location of M & M Equipment and Rental Company in 1971*

One of the employees was shop foreman Roscoe Anthony "Rock" White, a former Dallas policeman and United States Marine veteran. His work at the equipment company was primarily manual labor that offered him ample opportunity for reflection on his life and the troubling events of the past several months. Foremost among these was his attempt to change his lifestyle.

He especially wanted to rid himself of his "secret life," an affiliation with a covert organization he believed to be sanctioned by people high in the United States government.

Initially, White had been recruited into this world while in the military but had become disillusioned by the nature of the assignments given to him by his superiors.

Of special significance was his recent trip to Houston where Roscoe confronted other members of the covert group and informed them that he *"wanted out."* From that time forward, he knew that his life might be in danger and the thought weighed heavily on his mind as he and his co-worker, Dick Adair, went back to work.

The two men paused briefly at Roscoe's workbench as Adair excused himself to go to the restroom. As Adair walked away, Roscoe picked up a welding torch and lit it. Instantly there was an explosion with the force of the blast propelling Adair across the shop slamming him into the forklift. His lower torso and both legs were on fire. Soot and thick black smoke blanketed the entire shop. Seconds later, another explosion rocked the shop, and the entire work area was engulfed in a bright fireball.

A five-gallon container of highly flammable and corrosive chemical liquid had been overturned and ignited by the first explosion. The burning liquid was quickly spreading across the floor and streaming towards Roscoe. The fire quickly reached Roscoe's workbench and he was surrounded by a wall of fire.

Stumbling through the intense heat and smoke, Roscoe tried to find his way to the nearest exit. Upon reaching the door, he found it was locked tight. With his clothes and skin burning from the chemical, Roscoe was trapped in a wall of flame with no way out. His only hope was to reverse direction and try to run through the flames towards the open overhead door at the front of the shop. Staggering blindly through the chemical fire, he heard someone shouting, *"This way!"* Moving towards the voice, Roscoe could make out a tiny sliver of light from the overhead door. Seconds later, he stumbled into the parking lot.

In the swirling heat, smoke and fire, Roscoe saw a man running from the shop carrying a briefcase. He recognized the man and thought to himself, *"That's it, they got me."* At that point, he realized the fire was no accident, but a deliberate act and he was the intended target.

Still on fire, Roscoe staggered across the parking lot and away from the building. Falling to the ground he began rolling over and over in a desperate attempt to smother the flames. When the fire was extinguished, Roscoe got to his feet and stood naked in the parking lot waiting for the ambulance. The only article of clothing remaining was the thin leather belt wrapped around his waist and the soles of his work boots. His ears, nose and fingertips had been consumed by the flames and his entire body was charred black. Despite the severe injuries, he was calm and lucid as everyone waited for the ambulance. Remarkably, his sense of humor was intact, and he jokingly said to a co-worker, David A. David, *"Well, I guess this is gonna cost me my job."*

Neighboring businesses had already called the fire department and after an agonizing twenty minutes, two ambulances finally arrived; one for Roscoe the other for Adair whose injuries were less severe. The two men were quickly loaded into the ambulances and headed for Baylor Hospital, the nearest hospital to the business.

After the nine-mile trip through rush-hour traffic, the ambulances arrived at the emergency entrance. Once the nurses and attendants saw the extent of Roscoe's injuries, they informed the ambulance drivers that their facility was not equipped to deal with this level of trauma and suggested they be taken to Parkland Hospital. At that time, Parkland was one of the top burn centers in the South.

Learning he would be taken to Parkland; Roscoe felt a strong sense of irony. He knew from his training as a police officer that victims of severe chemical burns like his almost never survived. Even if he did live through the ordeal, the initial shock of being burned alive and the risk of infection typically sped up the process of death.

As he contemplated his certain fate, he thought it was somewhat appropriate he should die at Parkland – the very same hospital where President Kennedy died.

It was only eight years ago when President Kennedy was rushed to Parkland following the shooting in Dealey Plaza. Two days after the assassination, Lee Harvey Oswald was taken to Parkland after being shot by nightclub owner and FBI informant, Jack Ruby. On January 3, 1967, Ruby himself was admitted to the same hospital and died of coronary thrombosis after being diagnosed with cancer. Now the fourth figure with a connection to the assassination would likely die at the same hospital. As the ambulances made their way to the hospital, Roscoe may have thought, *"It's come full circle."*

Roscoe had known Jack Ruby and was a regular at the Carousel Club for several months prior to Kennedy's arrival in Dallas. In September of 1963, Ruby hired Roscoe's wife, Geneva, to work as a hostess at the club. Roscoe also knew Lee Harvey Oswald and was briefly stationed with him at the secret military and CIA base at Atsugi, Japan.

**Interestingly, in the months preceding the assassination, Oswald frequented the Carousel Club and Ruby introduced him to some of his entertainers as, "*My friend Lee of the CIA.*"**

Upon arrival at Parkland, Roscoe was quickly unloaded from the ambulance and taken immediately into the emergency room. There, a preliminary examination revealed that Roscoe had received third-degrees burns over his entire body.

Despite his horrific injuries, Roscoe was conscious and calmly provided information as the nurse completed the necessary medical forms. When he coughed, a black sooty substance spewed forth from his mouth. When Geneva White received the emergency call from the hospital, she was terrified. She was aware that during the past few months her husband had grown increasingly edgy and quick to anger and seemed preoccupied by some personal dilemma that caused him to fear for his life. Now she feared the worst – and with good reason.

Several months earlier, while attending a cosmetics convention in New Orleans, Geneva was approached by a man whom she had never met; he asked to speak to her privately. The man knew who she was and provided intimate details about her, her husband, and her children. The stranger, whose name she recalled was "Nick," demanded she take a message back to Roscoe who he referred to as *"Mandarin."*

She was to tell her husband that *"they"* had another assignment for him, and they were not going to let him *"get out."* The man told her, *"Rock has 48 hours to get in touch with me or else."*

Back in Dallas, before leaving for the hospital, Geneva made arrangements for a neighbor to stay with the boys while another neighbor drove her to the hospital. Later, when she realized her husband was unlikely to live, Geneva contacted the neighbor and requested that Tony and Ricky be brought to the hospital to see their father.

Just as the boys arrived at the emergency entrance, their father was being wheeled out on a gurney. Both boys cried out, *"Daddy, Daddy!"* Before being taken to a room, Roscoe asked to speak privately with his sons. He told them, *"...be good and take care of your mother."* Then, he motioned for Ricky to come over to the side of the gurney and whispered, *"Ricky, listen to me; it's time for you to grow up, take care of your brother and mother. I want you to know this wasn't an accident."* Roscoe had confided in his youngest son because he was physically larger, stronger and more able than Tony, who was "sickly" and had been diagnosed with chronic and severe asthma since birth.

On May 16, 2018, the authors met Reverend Jack Shaw at this office in Dallas, Texas, and were provided this account of his relationship with Roscoe and Geneva White.

Reverend Shaw said he first met Roscoe and Geneva in 1970. Roscoe was working for Page's drug store at the time. And, Reverend Shaw was trying to establish and build a new church in Richardson, Texas. For several months, Shaw counseled the couple during an especially strained period of their marriage. He said he had been introduced to the couple by another member of his congregation and had contacted Roscoe at his job.

The Whites attended one of Shaw's services and enjoyed his sermon and met many of the other members of the congregation. The minister visited Roscoe and Geneva in their home on several occasions; later, both he and Geneva became Christians. Roscoe had been struggling to make a change in one area of his life. This conversion would represent one of the most difficult challenges he had ever faced. Braced by his newfound faith and his desire to change his personal philosophy, Roscoe was determined to change – no matter the consequences.

The entire family became active members of the church and attended services nearly every Sunday. Rev. Shaw was surprised one day when Roscoe came to him and announced he wanted to purchase $10,000 in church bonds to help with the construction of the new church. Even though he gratefully accepted the offer, he couldn't help but wonder how as an assistant manager of a small chain store could afford to offer such a large donation. (Note: The purchasing power of $10,000 is the equivalent of about $79,300 in 2023.) Money never seemed to be an issue for the Whites. They had just purchased a new home in an upscale section of Richardson, Texas; both he and Geneva owned late-model cars and owned a cabin at Lake Whitney, Texas.

In the evening on the day Roscoe was injured, the Rev. Shaw arrived at the hospital and went into Roscoe's hospital room. When he first entered the room, he was shocked to see the extent of Roscoe's injuries. Later, he described his injuries as *"hideous and shocking."* Rev. Shaw told the authors, "*He [Roscoe] was unrecognizable."*

Rev. Shaw recalled that Roscoe was lying on his back with his upper torso raised slightly to help him breathe. Except for the soles of his feet, Roscoe's entire body was charred black, swollen twice its normal size and covered with a thin mesh gauze under a heavy coating of white cream. His ears were only small spots on the sides of his head, his nose was missing, and both hands were curled into tight fists.

When asked for the details of what had happened, Roscoe replied in a whispered tone, *"Jack, I saw someone running from where I was working. I saw a can under the bench when I came back from my break...I know who it was running away; it wasn't an accident."* After pausing a moment, Roscoe continued, *"Jack, I want you to know that I forgive him for what he did...regardless of how this happened, it's alright; I forgive him."*

Knowing Roscoe had days or hours to live, Reverend Shaw asked, "*Is everything alright between you and God? Have you got things straight with the Lord?"* Roscoe replied, *"I've got that settled. I know I have done a lot of wrong in my life, things I'm ashamed of and I'm sorry for it; but I know God has forgiven me and wiped that slate clean. I just hope the people I wronged will forgive me."*

Roscoe then spoke lovingly of his wife and expressed remorse and regret for all the pain he had caused her over the years. He said he would never understand how she could forgive him, yet he knew she had.

Roscoe then told him, *"I served my country and I'm proud of my service to my country, but you know, in war, sometimes you have to do things you're not proud of – sometimes innocent people have to die. I've taken lives on foreign soil, and I've taken lives on American soil, always in the line of duty."* After a short pause, as if deep in thought, Roscoe admitted, *"I have sinned against my country."*

Reverend Shaw said he and Roscoe prayed together. After praying, Shaw saw tears in Roscoe's eyes, and he seemed to be at peace with himself and his God. Before Shaw left, Roscoe said, *"Brother Jack, will you do something for me? Tell my boys that whatever happens, I love them both. Tell them their dad loves them."*

A few minutes later, Roscoe fell asleep. This would be the last time Rev. Shaw would see Roscoe.

The following day, less than twenty-four hours after the explosion, Roscoe went into cardiac arrest and died. He joined the growing list of individuals with some connection to the assassination who met untimely, often violent deaths.

Name White, Roscoe Anthony

Case No. 1944-71-0813

DIAGNOSES:

1. Severe burns of the body (95%).
2. Pulmonary edema and congestion.
3. Laryngeal edema.
4. Generalized subcutaneous edema.
5. Bilateral pleural effusions.
6. Ascites.
7. Multiple escarotomies.
8. Glandular and stromal hyperplasia of the prostate.

CONCLUSION:

In our opinion Roscoe A. White died of severe burns of the body. No significant natural disease process was found at autopsy. No other injuries were disclosed.

Benjamin P. Love, M.D.
Associate Pathologist

William Q. Sturner, M.D.
Medical Examiner

Charles S. Petty, M.D.
Chief Medical Examiner

TOXICOLOGY:

Blood Bank Blood alcohol - negative
CO - 2% sat.

Protocol prepared by Vada L. McWilliams

Certified as true copy of report on file in the Dallas County Medical Examiners' Office. This report consists of 4 pages and 0 photographs

Notary Public in and for Dallas County, Texas

December 16, 1971
Date of certification

*Roscoe White autopsy results*

On Friday, September 24, 1971, Roscoe Anthony White was laid to rest with full military and masonic honors in the Field of Honor at Restland Memorial Park in Dallas. Ricky, now almost eleven years old, was amazed at the outpouring of attention being paid to his late father. He watched and listened as a squadron of jets roared overhead, followed by a 21-gun salute that echoed in the crisp fall air. A lone bugler played "Taps" as an honor guard escorted Ricky's father's flag-draped casket to its final resting place.

Standing there that day, Ricky said a tearful and final goodbye to the man he had loved and looked up to with respect and admiration. At that time, the young boy could not possibly have known or even imagined what future events would force him to confront his father's secret legacy – a legacy encompassing the dark mystery surrounding the assassination of President John F. Kennedy.

Dead men tell no tales – or do they?

*Roscoe White's headstone*

# CHAPTER TWO:
## The Long-Lost Footlocker

One of the pivotal moments in the Roscoe White story occurred when Ricky found his father's Marine Corps footlocker. Growing up he remembered seeing it in the garage at their house on Nottingham in Richardson, Texas, but neither he nor his brother were ever allowed to look inside.

In October 1982, Geneva's father, Weldon Toland, died and the funeral was held two days later. After the graveside service, the family returned to the Toland home in Paris, Texas. While most of the family gathered in the house, two of Ricky's cousins went to the small shed at the north edge of the property hoping to find some antiques and an old upright piano they remembered playing as children.

*Ricky White stands in front of the shed where his father's footlocker was found. Photo by authors.*

After entering the shed, they found that the old piano was covered with cobwebs and dirt and pushed up against one of the walls. Next to the piano, under several layers of cardboard and blankets, they discovered a green trunk with the name “Roscoe A. White 1666106” stenciled on the lid in white paint.

Even though some of the letters and numbers had faded, there was no doubt regarding who owned the trunk. Leaving the trunk in place, they called Ricky to come to the shed, and once he saw his father’s name painted across the top, he immediately claimed it. As Ricky dragged the footlocker from the shed, he wondered what treasures might be inside, not realizing the contents would forever change his life.

*Roscoe White’s Marine Corps footlocker.*
*Photo courtesy of Ricky White.*

Surprisingly, the trunk was not locked, and when Ricky opened it, he saw a short-sleeved silk bowling shirt stitched with his father's first name in gold thread over the left breast pocket.

The back of the shirt identified the team's name and Roscoe's Marine Corps unit. In the bottom of the trunk, Ricky found his father's "swagger stick." The "stick" was a thin wood shaft topped with an empty rifle casing and sergeant's emblem on one end and a hollowed-out rifle bullet at the other end.

Painted in gold letters along the shaft was Roscoe's name and military serial number and the locations where his father had visited during his time in the Marines: Hawaii, Mindoro, Formosa Straits, Midway, Japan, Philippines, Indonesia, Okinawa, and Wake Island.

Ricky also found a rifle bayonet and scabbard with "Okinawa 60-61" stenciled in white paint. Scattered in the bottom of the trunk were a large assortment of papers and photographs, Roscoe's military records, dozens of letters sent and received while he was overseas, and other personal items from his father's time in the Marines.

Ricky and Tricia decided to take the footlocker back to their home in Midland, Texas where they could examine the contents in private. After several attempts of trying to squeeze the footlocker into Tricia's new muscle car, they realized the car had not been designed to carry such a large item. Not wanting to leave the contents behind, Ricky and Tricia transferred everything from the footlocker into a suitcase they had brought on their trip to Paris. Once the footlocker was empty, they threw the suitcase into the car and started for home leaving the footlocker behind. A few weeks later, Ricky returned to his grandparents' home and retrieved the footlocker.

Arriving back in Midland, Ricky carried the suitcase into the house and placed it on top of the pool table in their game room. It had been a long day and neither of them felt like looking through the material. For Ricky, just knowing his father's belongings were safe was enough for now. Working full-time and raising two small children left little free time to look through the contents and the suitcase remained closed for nearly a year.

Eventually, Ricky and Tricia found time to examine the material. Several of the more intriguing items found in the footlocker were: (1) a small black book with a clasp, (2) a green Wynnewood State Bank bag containing two keys, (3) a chrome 2-shot derringer and, (4) a previously unseen third backyard photograph of Oswald. (Note: See photo next page.)

*Wynnewood State Bank bag: Courtesy of Ricky White.*

Other items included photos of Lee Oswald (including his official police mug shot) two backyard photos, a photo of Lee Oswald's autopsy, a photo from inside the "sniper's nest" of the Texas School Book Depository, individual photos of Jack Ruby and Officer Tippit, letters to and from Roscoe while he was in the Marines and numerous official crime scene photos of evidence recovered by the Dallas police.

Before the press conference in 1990, Ricky brought the items from the footlocker to the JFK Assassination Information Center so they could be photographed and inventoried.

*Contents of Roscoe White's footlocker. Photo courtesy of J. Gary Shaw. (Note: The question mark in the photo represents Roscoe White's missing diary.)*

**The Backyard Photos**

The Warren Commission knew of two photographs allegedly depicting Lee Oswald standing in the backyard at the Neely Street address. Commission Exhibit C133-A later appeared on the cover of the February 21, 1964, edition of *Life* magazine. The arrow on preceding page photo points to the previously unseen third backyard photo of Lee Oswald.

The Dallas police had at least one version of a backyard photo long before the photos were officially found on Saturday afternoon, the day <u>after</u> the assassination.

*Commission Exhibit C133-A.*

*Commission Exhibit C 133-B*

## The Third Oswald Photo

A governmental commission looking into the assassination of President Kennedy learned of this previously unknown third Oswald photograph and requested that they be allowed to examine it. Their investigation revealed that this third photograph was a first-generation print, indicating that at one time, the Dallas Police were in possession of the negative. However, the photo was not included in the evidence that was supposed to have been turned over to governmental authorities. The House Select Committee on Assassinations (HSCA) expressed little-to-no interest in this photo and the missing negative.

*An original copy of this third previously unseen backyard photo was found among Roscoe White's possessions.*

*DPD Detective Bobby Brown recreates the pose seen in the third backyard photo.*

On November 29, 1963, the Dallas police and the Secret Service went to 214 West Neely Street and took photos of the property, including a replication of the Oswald pose in the previously unknown photo of Oswald. The existence of this replicated photo proves they were aware of its existence. There is no acknowledgment anywhere in the official record of this photo, only the recreated pose. The withholding of this photo from the official record appears to have been a deliberate decision. Why would they withhold the existence of this photo? The reasoning behind this mysterious (suspicious?) action has never been explained.

*A Dallas Police created "cut-out" template of the third backyard photo.*

The black book, as it turned out, was his father's diary that contained his written confessions about his involvement in the assassination of President Kennedy. These words shocked Ricky to his very core.

The keys from the bank bag led Ricky on a futile quest for what he hoped might be savings left for the family by his deceased father.

Ricky had no idea that the discovery of his father's footlocker would lead to the journey of a lifetime.

***"If you want to see the truth, you must be brave enough to look for it."***

***— Will Rogers***

# CHAPTER THREE:

## The Bank Bag, Two Keys, and A Secret Safe Deposit Box

Another item found in the footlocker was a green zippered bank bag imprinted with the words, "Wynnewood State Bank, Wynnewood Village, Dallas, Texas," and the bank's logo.

*Wynnewood State Bank bag and keys.*
*Courtesy of Ricky White.*

Inside the bag were two (2) silver keys with the following notations:

Key # 1 – Sargent & Greenleaf, Inc., Rochester, N.Y. USA F 91 411
Key # 2 – Mosler H000353 on one side and 203 on the reverse side.

*Close-up of the keys*

One branch of this bank was in the Wynnewood Village Shopping Center in Oak Cliff. Ricky said his father's diary mentioned a large amount of money being kept in a safe deposit box but did not identify the bank. Since each key was stamped with different notations, Ricky wondered if these keys might be for _two_ different safe deposit boxes. Since the keys were found inside a bank bag from Wynnewood State Bank, Ricky naturally assumed the keys were for two different boxes at that bank.

On September 28, 1987, Ricky and Geneva arrived unannounced at the Oak Cliff branch of Wynnewood Bank at 731 West Illinois Street. After showing identification and Roscoe's death certificate, they were escorted into the vault. Using the key stamped with the number #203 (the Mosler key) the bank representative verified the key was for a box in their vault. However, the other key from the bank bag did not correspond to any safe deposit boxes at the branch.

*Vault inside Wynnewood State Bank*

With the key from the bank and the master key, box # 203 was opened. Once opened, Ricky told the authors, *"It was plum full of bearer bonds."* The bank representative removed the box's contents one at a time and placed them on top of a table in the vault but neither Geneva nor Ricky was permitted to handle the bonds.

As the bonds were being counted, Ricky remembers the bank employee remained in the vault and wrote an inventory of the bonds along with each bond's denomination. After the bonds were counted, the bank employee gave a handwritten receipt to Geneva. Eventually, Ricky gave this receipt to Larry Howard at the JFK Assassination Information Center (JFKAIC). Ricky remembers the receipt showed the bonds totaled two hundred thousand dollars ($200,000) or two-hundred and fifty thousand dollars ($250,000). The current location of the receipt, if it still exists, is unknown.

Ricky and Geneva were not allowed to leave with the bonds until they could show proof that Roscoe's will had been through probate.

Because neither Ricky nor Geneva had money to hire an attorney, Ricky contacted Midland County Assistant District Attorney Al W. Schorre, Jr. On November 13, 1987, Ricky met with Schorre at his office and told him how he came in possession of the keys, and that his father had been a Dallas police officer and participated in the Kennedy assassination. Ricky remembers providing Schorre with the name and location of the bank. However, he did not mention what was inside the safe deposit box or that he and his mother had previously visited the bank.

*Midland County Assistant District Attorney Al W. Shorre.*

*Midland Investigator J. D. Luckie*

After the meeting, Schorre told Ricky that he was interested in helping and assigned his investigator J. D. Luckie to look into the matter. After Ricky left the office, Schorre contacted the Midland FBI office and told them of his meeting with Ricky. This was when the FBI took an immediate interest in Ricky and Tricia.

At their first meeting, Schorre had agreed to help but had done very little investigation and Ricky became frustrated by the lack of progress. Ricky told the authors that *"Schorre kept dragging his feet and he wasn't helping us."* (R. White, video interview, April 28, 2018.)

On December 30, 1987, Luckie contacted Corporal Jack Beavers of the Dallas Police Department's Intelligence Unit and requested information about Ricky's father. Luckie told Beavers that Ricky had contacted the District Attorney's Office in Midland and told them of the existence of a safe deposit box containing $200,000 in cash <u>and</u> a diary implicating his father, a former DPD officer, in the Kennedy assassination. Luckie also told Beavers that Ricky's father knew Lee Harvey Oswald. (Source: Dallas Police Department "SECRET" memo from Cpl. Beavers to Capt. W. R. Rollins.) This memo was not released to the public until 1998.

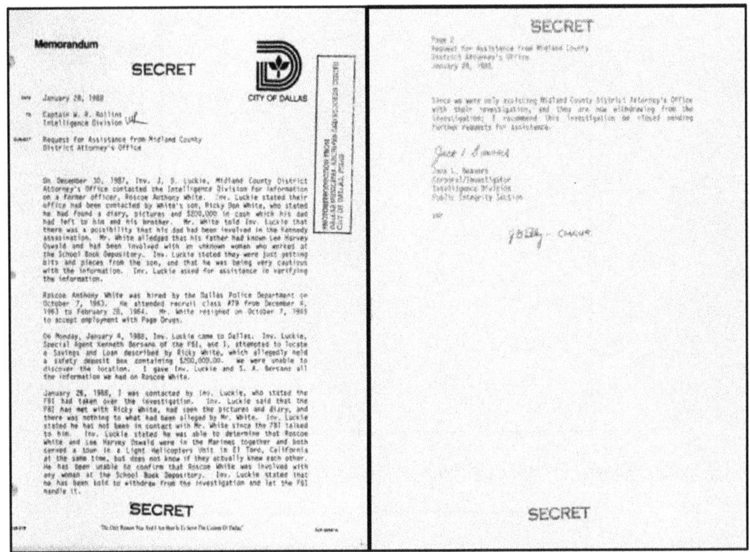

Memorandum

SECRET

CITY OF DALLAS

January 28, 1988

Captain W. R. Rollins
Intelligence Division

Request for Assistance from Midland County
District Attorney's Office

On December 30, 1987, Inv. J. S. Luckie, Midland County District Attorney's Office contacted the Intelligence Division for information on a former officer, Roscoe Anthony White. Inv. Luckie stated their office had been contacted by White's son, Ricky Don White, who stated he had found a diary, pictures and $200,000 in cash which his dad had left to him and his brother. Mr. White told Inv. Luckie that there was a possibility that his dad had been involved in the Kennedy assassination. Mr. White alledged that his father had known Lee Harvey Oswald and had been involved with an unknown woman who worked at the School Book Depository. Inv. Luckie stated they were just getting bits and pieces from the son, and that he was being very cautious with the information. Inv. Luckie asked for assistance in verifying the information.

Roscoe Anthony White was hired by the Dallas Police Department on October 7, 1963. He attended recruit class #79 from December 4, 1963 to February 28, 1964. Mr. White resigned on October 7, 1965 to accept employment with Page Drugs.

On Monday, January 4, 1988, Inv. Luckie came to Dallas. Inv. Luckie, Special Agent Kenneth Bersano of the FBI, and I, attempted to locate a Savings and Loan described by Ricky White, which allegedly held a safety deposit box containing $200,000.00. We were unable to discover the location. I gave Inv. Luckie and S. A. Bersano all the information we had on Roscoe White.

January 26, 1988, I was contacted by Inv. Luckie, who stated the FBI had taken over the investigation. Inv. Luckie said that the FBI had met with Ricky White, had seen the pictures and diary, and there was nothing to what had been alleged by Mr. White. Inv. Luckie stated he has not been in contact with Mr. White since the FBI talked to him. Inv. Luckie stated he was able to determine that Roscoe White and Lee Harvey Oswald were in the Marines together and both served a tour in a Light Helicopters Unit in El Toro, California at the same time, but does not know if they actually knew each other. He has been unable to confirm that Roscoe White was involved with any woman at the School Book Depository. Inv. Luckie stated that he has been told to withdraw from the investigation and let the FBI handle it.

SECRET

SECRET

Page 2
Request for Assistance from Midland County
District Attorney's Office
January 28, 1988

Since we were only assisting Midland County District Attorney's Office with their investigation, and they are now withdrawing from the investigation, I recommend this investigation be closed pending further requests for assistance.

Jack L. [illegible]
Corporal/Investigator
Intelligence Division
Public Integrity Section

SECRET

*SECRET memo (page 1)* *SECRET memo (page 2)*

On December 31, 1987, the day after Luckie contacted the DPD Intelligence Unit, Special Agents Thomas N. Farris and Edward M. Stroz from the El Paso FBI field office, and John K. Hicks from the Midland field office began covert surveillance on the couple. Surveillance began at 7 a.m. and terminated at 12:30 p.m. When the authors showed Ricky this FBI document, he believed the surveillance was directly related to his meeting with Al Schorre. It is unclear on whose orders – or why – the surveillance was initiated.

FD-340 (Rev. 4-3-84)

Field File No. EP 89A 52 – 1A(13)
OO and File No.
Date Received 12/31/87
From Thomas N. Farris + Edw. Stroz
(Name of Contributor)
FBI
(Address of Contributor)
(City and State)
By
(Name of Special Agent)
To Be Returned ☐ Yes ☑ No Receipt Given ☐ Yes ☑ No
Grand Jury Material - Disseminate Only Pursuant to Rule 6(e), Federal Rules of Criminal Procedure ☐ Yes ☑ No
Title:
ALL INFORMATION CONTAINED in this envelope HEREIN IS UNCLASSIFIED DATE 10-15-93 BY 9803RDD/KSR
Reference:
(Communication Enclosing Material) JFK
Description: ☐ Original notes re interview of
Surveillance log: 12/31/87 @ 302 [illegible] D. Midland + following.
DO NOT DESTROY PENDING LITIGATION

*Cover page of surveillance log for December 31, 1987.*

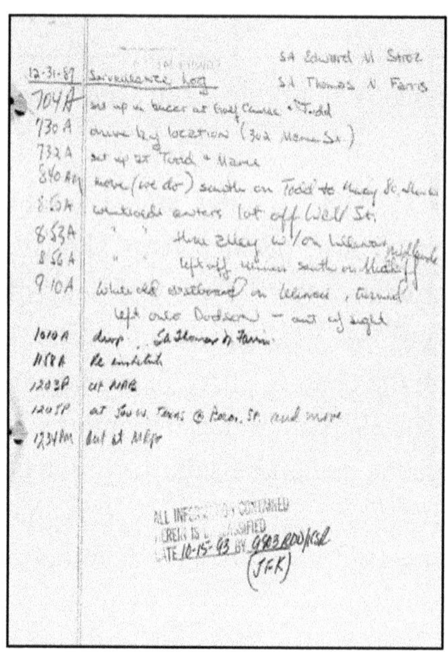

12-31-87 Surveillance Log SA Edward M. Stroz SA Thomas N. Farris
704A set up in [illegible] at Golf Course + Todd
730A drive by location (302 [illegible] St.)
732A set up at Todd + [illegible]
840A move (we do) south on Todd to [illegible]
853A [illegible] enters lot off Wall St.
853A [illegible] alley w/on Illinois
856A left off [illegible] south on Midland
910A [illegible] eastbound on Illinois, turned left onto Dodson – out of sight
1010A [illegible] SA Thomas N. Farris
1158A [illegible]
1203P at MAR
1205P at [illegible] Texas @ [illegible] St. and [illegible]
1234PM out at [illegible]
ALL INFORMATION CONTAINED HEREIN IS UNCLASSIFIED DATE 10-15-93 BY 9803RDD/KSR (JFK)

*Surveillance Log, December 31, 1987*

At this time, the Bureau had only heard about the alleged existence of the assassination-related materials and information said to be in Ricky's possession. Such an immediate, uneasiness and intense interest concerning this material is puzzling.

The authors obtained numerous FBI memos documenting the Bureau's interest in the couple. The first memo dated January 1988 was sent to Deputy Assistant Director Bob A. Ricks with the General Government Crimes Unit, White Collar Crimes Section (Note: Ricks was the agent in charge of the siege at Waco in 1993 and the lead agent in the Oklahoma Bombing investigation in 1995). In this memo, the agents summarized their activities.

One memo reads:

> *In conjunction with Midland County District Attorney's office, on December 31, 1987, El Paso FBI established early morning surveillance of Ricky Don White's residence at 302 Marie Drive, Midland, Texas.*
>
> *Al W. Schorre, Jr., the Midland County District Attorney, had previously made arrangements with White to telephone him on January 2, 1988. It was decided to re-establish surveillance and have Schorre call White at 2:00 p.m. and was stalled until about 4:00 p.m.*

On January 2, 1988, FBI Special Agents John Hicks and Edward Storz continued surveillance on the couple from

1:45 p.m. until 4:25 p.m. On this date, a memo was submitted detailing the day's activities:

> *At about 8:40 p.m., January 2, 1988, Schorre contacted Special Agent Thomas N. Farris and advised he had talked with White at about 8:30 p.m. Schorre was told to come to the White's home in the morning (January 3, 1988). Schorre was given the address and directions to the house. Schorre had told White it would be after church, but it was decided to show up at White's door at about 10:00 a.m. on January 3, 1988. At about 10:30 a.m., January 3, 1988, Schorre and his investigator J. D. Luckie, appeared on White's front porch and were admitted. There ensued an hour and a half interview. Afterwards, Schorre and Luckie provided the following concerning their meeting.*
>
> *Tricia White is fully aware of what is happening. She has recently done a good deal of reading about the assassination. Schorre and Luckie observed Ector County library books in the residence. El Paso will continue to follow this matter closely and anticipates an early* <u>*confrontational interview*</u> *by the FBI once White has been provided the opportunity to produce the contents of the safety deposit box."* [emphasis added]
>
> *The entire White family is concerned about publicity in this matter and does not want to make their information public. There are leery of expanding contact with law enforcement, especially to the FBI.*

> *Roscoe White's widow and Ricky's mother, Geneva Galle (White) had the military locker in her possession and still has it. The 'diary" consists of a smaller three-ring looseleaf notebook in which White had written things that happened to him as a Dallas police officer.*
>
> *Other things found in the locker are a large quantity of newspapers from the Dallas area reporting the assassination, the photographs and the offense report. Mrs. Galle does not want anything to do with this matter and does not want contact with law enforcement.*
>
> *Roscoe Anthony "Tony" White is the older brother of Ricky White and lives in Lubbock, Texas. He has taken and failed the CPA examination on three occasions. Tony White has the "diary" in his possession at this time. Tony and the mother are displeased with Ricky for his disclosures to the district attorney.*

The above description concerning the diary is one more example of the FBI's constant, almost desperate denial of its existence. The statement that Tony White is in possession of the diary is false. Ricky categorically denied that his brother ever saw the diary, and in fact, he never wanted to be included in Ricky's interest in his father's life.

The statement that Tricia *"...has recently done a good deal of reading about the assassination"* is a total fabrication. Prior to Schorre's visit, neither Tricia nor Ricky had ever read ANY books on the assassination. This was just another example of the FBI's deceptive, self-serving practices. One wonders how illegal the FBI thought it was that the White's had *"...Ector County library books in the residence?"*

The FBI's intense interest in the materials left behind by Roscoe flies in the face of their constant, almost desperate, denial of an accomplice or accomplices in the President's assassination.

Too, the act that the FBI was looking forward to a "confrontational" (threatening) interview with Ricky also speaks volumes about their bullying and browbeating tactics concerning the Roscoe White revelations.

The FBI continued its surveillance of the Whites on January 2, 1988, and discontinued surveillance on January 3, 1988.

Field File No.

OO and File No.

Date Received 1-2-88

From

(Name of Contributor)

(Address of Contributor)

ALL INFORMATION CONTAINED

(City and State)

By 10-15-93

(Name of Special Agent)

To Be Returned ☐ Yes ☐ No Receipt Given ☐ Yes ☐ No

Grand Jury Material - Disseminate Only Pursuant to Rule 6(e), Federal Rules of Criminal Procedure ☐ Yes ☐ No

Title: DO NOT DESTROY - PRESERVE FOR SELECT COMMITTEE ON ASSASSINATIONS

Reference: (Communication Enclosing Material)

Description: ☐ Original notes re interview of

DO NOT DESTROY - PENDING LITIGATION

*Cover page of surveillance log for January 2, 1988.*

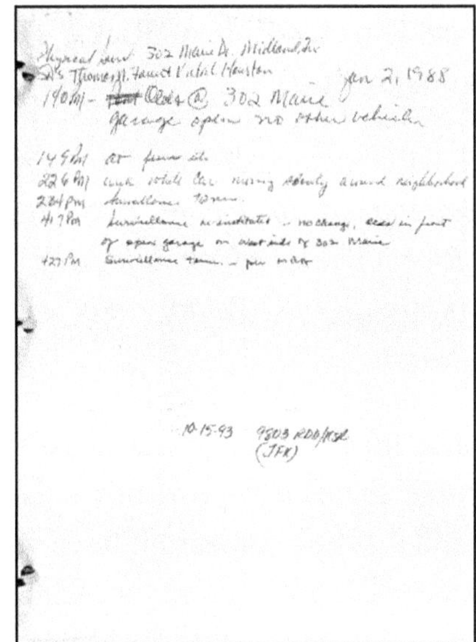

*Surveillance notes, January 2, 1988*

**The Hunt for the Elusive Safe Deposit Box Continues**

On the last page of this FBI memo from January 1988, SA Butler wrote, *"The safety deposit box in Oakcliff [sp] Texas, was actually bought for $3,000 by Roscoe White, Sr. in 1968 and not 1964 as previously reported."* Apparently, the FBI was able to locate the safe deposit box, as well as its rental history, without the knowledge and assistance of the Whites. And, the bearer bonds, like the diary, disappeared.

The next day, Monday, January 4, 1988, Luckie returned to the Dallas Police Department where he met Beavers and FBI Special Agent Kenneth Bersano of the Dallas FBI field office. Together, the three men attempted to locate the bank where Ricky had told them his father kept a safe deposit box. On this same date, a completely redacted FBI "PRIORITY" teletype was sent from "FBI Dallas" to "Director, FBI Deputy Assistant Director Bob A. Ricks." The content of this teletype is unknown.

In the SECRET DPD memo submitted by Corporal Beavers, he wrote *"...attempted to locate a Savings and Loan described by Ricky White which allegedly held a safety deposit box containing $200,000. We were unable to discover the location."*

This memo, unless the FBI again made a false statement, was positive proof that the safe deposit box existed in Roscoe White's name and that he purchased it three years before his death. That Roscoe "bought" this box for $3,000 seems to be highly unusual -- if not unheard of. One reasonable explanation the authors can envision is that Roscoe believed he might need the box for an extended period.

**Ricky Seeks Additional Counsel**

In the first week of January 1988, Ricky – frustrated by Schorre's lack of progress in the matter – sought additional help from a friend. Ricky confided parts of the story to his friend and asked for help. The friend became so concerned about Ricky that he immediately contacted Jerry Smith, an attorney friend in Hereford, Texas. Smith called Ricky the following evening and they agreed to meet at his home on January 12. Before Smith arrived at the Whites' home, Ricky laid out all the material on the pool table except for the diary.

When Smith arrived, Ricky showed him all his father's assassination-related materials, briefly mentioned the diary's existence, and verbally summarized his father's entry for November 22, 1963. After about three hours with Ricky and Tricia, Smith returned to Hereford.

J. Gary Shaw, summarizes this meeting:

> *Smith said Ricky was "spooked" and "moved" as he displayed and discussed his father's belongings, which were spread out on top of a pool table in the den of his home. Ricky told him* [Smith] *how he came into possession of the materials and remembers seeing a small brown shopping bag containing letters written to and from Roscoe during the period of his military service. There was also a series of photographs, apparently taken by Ricky's father while in the Marines, as well as his military records. Other photographs were clearly related to the Kennedy assassination. These*

> *included one, or perhaps two, of Lee Oswald holding a firearm and interior and exterior scenes of the Texas School Book Depository building. The most critical piece of materials, Smith recalls, was a bank record of some kind which showed a deposit of $800,000, along with a key; these were in a money bag and contained a notation with numbers on it.* [Note: Ricky says the deposit record was for a sum of $200,000, not $800,000.]

Ricky told Smith that the most important thing was his father's diary. Smith said Ricky became quite emotional as he recalled his father's words: *"Three people shooting; father fired from grassy knoll; was working for Dallas Police. Tippit was not directly involved but was killed by his father."*

Ricky asked what Smith thought the best course of action would be concerning the diary. Smith suggested that multiple copies be made immediately and that he (Smith) be allowed to keep one copy in his office safe. Ricky said he would discuss it with his family and let Smith know.

<u>As if on cue, the very next day FBI agents swept in and Roscoe's diary disappeared – never to be seen again.</u>

It was later learned that it was the Midland County Assistant District Attorney Al Schorre who first notified the FBI about Ricky, <u>not</u> Jerry Smith.

**Anxious Bureau Agents Barge In**

The next day, two men arrived unannounced at Ricky and Tricia's home in Midland, Texas. The White's babysitter, Denise Carter, greeted the men who identified themselves as FBI agents, Thomas N. Farris and Ronald Butler from the Midland field office. They informed Ms. Carter that they needed to talk to Ricky "immediately" and directed her to call Ricky and tell him that they were there and that he must return home as soon as possible.

When Ricky arrived at the house he was met by the agents in the front yard. They informed him that the purpose of their visit was to discuss certain materials in his possession that belonged to his late father, Roscoe White. The agents were primarily interested in the safe deposit box keys.

Before entering the house, SA Butler initiated the conversation by directing Ricky to read aloud from a United States Criminal Code book. Ricky remembers reading a section stating that withholding evidence in an ongoing investigation could result in a fine of $100,000 and/or imprisonment for up to ten years.

The aggressive and intimidating manner in which the agents confronted Ricky validated the January 1988 FBI memo which stated that they "*...anticipated an early <u>confrontational interview</u> by the FBI...*"

Ricky telephoned Tricia's cousin, an attorney, who advised that he should fully cooperate with the agents. Reluctantly, Ricky allowed the two agents into his house where he was directed to pack all his father's assassination-related material into a box and accompany them to their offices in downtown Midland. Ms. Carter helped Ricky transfer the material, including the diary, from the suitcase into a cardboard box. Ricky placed the box in his car and followed the agents to their office.

Ricky was taken to an upper floor of the Federal Building and led into a secure room. There, he noted that the agents seemed to show significantly more interest in the safe deposit box keys. The FBI likely believed there was something significant in the deposit box. Shortly after Roscoe died in 1971, two men approached Roscoe's half-brother and asked if he had received any books or packages from Roscoe before he died. (Source: Isaac Walton Rogers to J. Gary Shaw, 7/13/90). Perhaps they were still in search of these obviously important "books or packages."

At one point during the interrogation, Ricky witnessed Agent Farris making clay impressions of both keys.

While Butler questioned Ricky, Farris made copies of almost everything found in the box, including several pages from the diary. Ricky said there was no copy machine in the room but watched as Farris scanned select pages from the diary using a "hand wand" device.

Butler accused Ricky's father of being a thief who stole this material from the Dallas Police Department. Understandably, Butler denied ever seeing or copying the diary.

In response, Ricky pointed out that the agents read aloud the November 22, 1963, diary entry to which Butler remarked, *"These entries are insane . . . your father had a fanciful imagination."* (Source: R. White, video interview, April 28, 2018)

During the interview, Ricky recalled seeing a speakerphone on the table. One of the agents told him that the man on the phone was "*...a Senator from Pennsylvania,"* but did not identify him by name. (Note: In 1988, Arlen Specter was the Senator from Pennsylvania who had been one of the staff attorneys assigned to the Warren Commission. Specter is also known for developing, promoting, and defending the absurd single-bullet theory.)

After five agonizing hours, the agents finally told Ricky he was free to leave. Both agents stayed in the room as Ricky transferred all the material, <u>including the diary</u>, back into the cardboard box.

After returning home, Ricky placed the cardboard box on top of the pool table in their game room, went to the bedroom, and laid across the bed. Emotionally and physically drained, he began to weep.

Later, after Tricia arrived home from work, she heard a knock at the front door. Standing at the front door was Agent Farris who explained to her he thought Ricky had accidentally picked up his notebook along with his father's materials. Tricia then went to the bedroom door, told Ricky the agent was there, and that he wanted to retrieve it. Ricky told her that the material was on the pool table in the game room and that the agent could get it. As Tricia went back to tell the agent where the box was located, he was already heading for the front door. She remembers that the agent had nothing in his hands, and said as he slipped past her, *"I got what I needed, thanks."*

**More Bank Visits**

Between September 1987 and January 1991, Ricky made three more visits to Wynnewood State Bank, now operating under the name, Continental Bank, hoping to retrieve the contents of his father's safe deposit box.

On March 7, 1989, Ricky and his friend, Andy Burke visited the bank. However, they were denied access to the box by the bank officials who informed them they needed to contact the local FBI office for additional information. Ricky now realized that the FBI was involved and the clay impressions they made in January 1988 may have been used to make keys to open the box.

After leaving the bank, Ricky and Andy went to the FBI field office in Dallas and spoke with Special Agents Paul Shannon and Gary L. Gerszewski. Ricky and Andy tell the agents that they have "new" information on the Kennedy assassination. The FBI discounts their story, and in a memo written that same day, the agents wrote:

> *"...White and Burke had visited CONTINENTAL BANK, formerly WYNNEWOOD STATE BANK of Oak Cliff, Texas. They had been unsuccessful in locating the safe deposit boxes through the bank and stated they wanted the FBI to find the boxes for them and then share with them the contents."*

On the last page of this FBI memo, the agents wrote:

> *"...it was clear the RICKY WHITE'S claim had been discounted. WHITE, in fact, had admitted he fabricated much of his story and was attempting to sell it to television networks. In view of the following and the behavior of BURKE and WHITE in the interview, the interviewing agents and SSRA RON BUTLER opined that the two visited the FBI specifically to gain admission of some sort that they could then use to either buttress their theory or claim an FBI coverup. In view of the following Dallas is conducting no investigation into this matter."*

To be factual, Ricky never admitted that he "*...fabricated much of his story."* And there was never an attempt to sell the story to the television networks. The statement that the Bureau was *"...conducting no investigation into this matter"* is revealing to say the least.

The mindset of the agents as seen in the above memo perfectly illustrates the FBI's attitude toward inconvenient information or witnesses in the JFK case. As Sylvia Meagher writes in <u>Accessories After the Fact,</u> "*...the FBI's treatment of bothersome witnesses in this case were met with extreme bias, incompetence, carelessness and irrefutable instances of outright hostility and dishonesty."*

In 1990, Ricky and Texas Certified Legal Investigator Joe West visited the Continental Bank. After several minutes of discussion with a bank employee, the men were allowed into the vault but were told that the key would not open the box.

Ricky made one final visit to the bank with Texas Attorney General (TAG) Investigator Ned Butler in January 1991. Upon arrival, the bank manager – whom Ricky and his mother dealt with previously – was summoned to the bank. The manager provided Butler with a list of the previous owners of Box 203; all the names were "whited out." After leaving the bank, Butler scraped the "white-out" off the page and noticed that one of the previous owners was formerly involved in money laundering.

The manager told them that the black dot notation next to certain names on the list indicated that the person was deceased. For that reason, they would not be allowed to use the key to open the box. While Ricky and Butler were at the bank, the manager made two telephone calls to unknown numbers. Later, Butler told Ricky that he felt the bank manager was hiding something.

As of this date, the disposition of the bearer bonds in safe deposit box # 203, originally seen by Ricky at Wynnewood State Bank in 1987, is unknown.

***"Justice will not be served until those who are unaffected are as outraged as those who are."***

***— Benjamin Franklin***

# CHAPTER FOUR:
## The FBI and the "Missing" Diary

Keeping a handwritten record of one's intimate thoughts with the intention of it remaining private is generally not an activity undertaken by the typical American male. Most men have neither the desire nor propensity to record their innermost thoughts and feelings on paper. Although a diary may provide information for a memoir or future autobiography – it is generally written for the author's sole use.

*Assassins and their diaries.*

Throughout history, there are many examples of the famous and infamous keeping a permanent record of their daily activities. When the term, "keeping a diary" is mentioned, a typical assumption would be an activity reserved for young girls writing about their current or former boyfriends, their dreams for the future or to keep secrets from family members.

Historically, not all men who kept a written record of their exploits have accomplished great deeds; some were criminals who felt compelled to document their deeds. Four of history's more infamous assassins kept diaries which were later found among their possessions. Additionally, other notable personalities and celebrities have been known to record their most intimate experiences and thoughts.

It's significant that Roscoe White also kept a diary.

**John Wilkes Booth's Diary**

John Wilkes Booth shot and killed President Abraham Lincoln and was then shot to death twelve days later by his captors. His diary, written after the assassination, contained repeated use of the plurals "we" and "our." Though the diary was in the hands of the government at the time of Booth's trial, it was not introduced into evidence.

Two years after the trial, the government admitted they had had Booth's diary all along but that now, it **had numerous pages cut from it. These pages have never been recovered.**

**Sirhan B. Sirhan's Diary**

In March 1968, Senator Robert Kennedy, President Kennedy's younger brother, announced his candidacy for President. On the night of June 5, having just won the California Democratic primary, the Senator was poised to become the party's nominee to run against Richard Nixon.

Unfortunately, Senator Kennedy would not live to fulfill his dream of occupying the White House. As he walked through the kitchen of the Ambassador Hotel, multiple shots were fired; two bullets struck Kennedy in the chest and head. The accused assassin was captured at the scene with a gun in hand and was later identified as a young Jordanian named Sirhan B. Sirhan.

After Sirhan's arrest, the Los Angeles Police Department found a "diary" at his mother's home in Pasadena, California. The "diary" contained numerous incoherent and repeating phrases. One such phrase was, "*My determination to eliminate RFK is becoming the more and more* [sic] *of an unshakable obsession,*" and "*RFK must die.*" These ramblings became part of the prosecution's key evidence in determining Sirhan's premeditation to kill Kennedy.

**Arthur Bremer's Diary**

The 1972 presidential election saw another Democrat muddy the political waters for Richard Nixon. This time it was southern right-wing conservative Governor George Wallace who threatened Nixon's reelection bid. Governor Wallace firmly opposed the civil rights movement (strong causes for both Kennedy brothers) and led both of his Democratic primary opponents in total votes. If Wallace did not get the nomination of his party, he could still be a strong third-party candidate, thereby draining many of the conservative votes from both the Republican and Democratic nominees. This was a major concern for the Nixon reelection team.

On May 15, 1972, unemployed busboy Arthur Herman Bremer attempted to assassinate Governor George Wallace of Alabama at a campaign stop in Laurel, Maryland. One of the bullets fired hit Wallace's spine, paralyzing him and forcing his withdrawal from the race. Subsequently, Richard Nixon was reelected in a landslide victory over Hubert Humphrey.

Bremer also kept a diary that was "conveniently" left in his car near the campaign rally. As with the Sirhan "diary," Bremer's journal became primary evidence at his trial. During the trial, in support of his not guilty plea by reason of insanity, the defense introduced into evidence a document identified by the FBI as "Manuscript Found in Bremer's Vehicle."

The manuscript consisted of the last 113 pages of a diary that Bremer kept for months. Allegedly, Bremer buried the first 148 pages somewhere near his furnished room in Milwaukee. Ironically, ex-CIA agent and Watergate burglar, E. Howard Hunt was ordered to travel to Bremer's apartment and plant documents linking him to the Democrats. Hunt did not make the trip because the FBI had moved in too quickly and sealed the apartment.

## Mary Pinchot Meyer's Diary

Mary Pinchot Meyer was the former wife of the CIA's Cord Meyer, creator of special covert operations through international groups, labor unions, authors, and publishers.

As one of JFK's several mistresses, she chronicled their affair in her diary. On October 12, 1964, while walking along the Chesapeake & Ohio Canal towpath near the Potomac River in Georgetown, two shots were heard, and two witnesses said they saw an African American man standing over her. Following her murder, which remains unsolved to this day, ***her diary was confiscated and allegedly destroyed*** by CIA Counterintelligence Chief, James Angleton.

## Marilyn Monroe's Diary

President Kennedy and his brother, U.S. Attorney General Robert Kennedy, were both having affairs with famed actress Marilyn Monroe. When the Kennedys cut off the liaisons, it was alleged that Monroe threatened to call a press conference to expose the affairs and other secrets. Allegedly, the diary contained tidbits gleaned from the Kennedy brother's details about the Bay of Pigs and the administration's attempts to assassinate Castro. ***Her diary has disappeared.***

## Allen Lawrence Pope's Diary

A noteworthy example of using a diary as protection can be found in the story of CIA contract agent and retired Air Force pilot, Allen Lawrence Pope. (Source: Prouty, Fletcher. *The Secret Team: The CIA and Its Allies in Control of the United States and the World.* Simon & Schuster, New York, NY, 1973, pp. 365-6.)

In 1958, Marine units in the Philippines and Okinawa were providing military support for a large-scale CIA operation against President Sukarno of Indonesia. The US government had supplied the right-wing rebel forces with arms and a small air force of B-26 bombers in an attempt to overthrow Sukarno. Interestingly, in March 1958, Marine Roscoe White departed Cubi Point (Subic Bay) in the Philippines for Okinawa and remained there until September 2, 1958.

On May 18, 1958, two months after White's unit arrived on Okinawa, Pope was flying a modified B-26 *Invader* under the cover of the CIA's Civil Air Transport (CAT) and was shot down by anti-aircraft fire. Pope had just completed a bombing run over Ambon City in eastern Indonesia. The run destroyed an open market and a church and casualties included civilians and military personnel. Pope and his crew of mixed nationalities were taken prisoners. The Indonesians found Pope's logbook, a diary, and identification that verified his employment by the CIA.

The United States categorically denied providing any support to anti-Sukarno forces. In business-as-usual fashion, *The New York Times* published numerous articles condemning the Indonesians for circulating false reports about the U.S. giving aid to the rebels. This pattern was used again in the U-2 affair and later during the Bay of Pigs fiasco. The phrase "categorically deny" would again manifest itself during the FBI's outrageous handling of Roscoe White's diary.

Why would a man flying a clandestine mission for an American intelligence agency carry compromising identification on his person? Perhaps the answer is – survival. It is not uncommon for an intelligence operative to take such precautionary steps to protect himself in the event of capture.

The example of Pope's diary makes the existence and importance of the Roscoe White diary even more plausible.

**Lee Harvey Oswald's Diary**

After Oswald's arrest, his diary was found and identified as the "Historical Diary" by *Life* magazine. Document experts determined that the entire diary bore all the markings of fabrication; of primary importance was the determination that it appeared to have been written in one or two sittings long after the events occurred. If the diary was indeed fake, the reason behind its creation has eluded researchers to this day.

There were other writings in addition to the diary. One example is particularly noteworthy because it provided a glimpse into the writer's mind as he considered the prospect of an American coup d'etat – the overthrow of the American Government.

The referenced writing, Commission Exhibit 102, is listed as "Notes for a speech" in the Warren Commission. It is printed here verbatim with incorrect spelling and punctuation.

It reads:

*"speech before"*

*"Americans are apt to scoff at the idea, that a coup in the US., as so often happens in Latin American countries, could ever replace our government. but that is an idea that has grounds for consideration. Which military organization has the potentialities of executing such action? Is it the army? With is many constripes, its unwieldy size its scores of bases scattered across the world? The case of Gen. Walker shows that an army, at least, is not fertail enough ground for a far right regime to go a very long way. for the same reasons of size and desposition the Navy and air force is also to be more or less disregarded. Which service then, can qwalify to launch a coup in the USA? Small size, a permanent hard core of officers and few baseis is necscary. Only one outfit fits that description and the U.S.M.C. is a right wing infiltrated organization of dire potential consequence's to the freedoms of the U.S. I agree with former President Truman when he said that The Marine Corps should be abolished'.*

**Roscoe White's Diary**

The day Ricky found his father's diary in 1982 was an important moment. The writings within this small book would forever change his life. Based upon the authorities' past experiences that involved the above-mentioned diaries, it is not surprising that Roscoe White's diary also disappeared. Several family members recall seeing Roscoe occasionally writing in the small black book – a book no one else was ever allowed to read.

Ricky told the authors that when the family lived at 727 Nottingham in Richardson, his father enclosed a small section of the garage as his own private workroom. The door to this space was secured with a heavy padlock and was strictly *". . . off limits to the rest of us."* (Source: R. White, personal communication, April 28, 2018.)

*727 Nottingham, Richardson, Texas 2021.*

Occasionally, when Ricky and his brother were nearby, they were able to get a brief glimpse into the private workshop as their father entered or exited. Ricky said that the workshop housed a photo enlarger and bullet reloading equipment atop a small workbench. He remembered seeing the footlocker on the floor next to the workbench and later believed that his father kept the diary in the footlocker.

Several years after Ricky found the footlocker, he finally took time to focus on the little black book's contents. Ricky described the book as having a cheap black binding and was about six inches by eight inches in size. The cover was well worn, but the rest of the book was in good condition. Opening the book, Ricky immediately recognized his father's distinct handwriting. He said there were no pre-printed dates on its pages, only horizontal lines across the pages, much like a piece of notebook paper.

As Ricky read the first dozen pages, he quickly realized that his father used the little book as a diary that documented his time in the Marine Corps. Written in pencil, the entries chronicled important events in his father's life beginning in February 1957, when he enlisted in the Marines, and concluded with his final entry on September 20, 1971 – three days before his tragic death.

As one who had never been an avid reader of anything, Ricky found reading the little black book difficult on several fronts; namely, his father's use of military jargon was unfamiliar to him and some of the writing had faded, which made it even more difficult to read.

As he read, Ricky noticed a recurring pattern in his father's writing; the names of other soldiers were never used, only dates, places, and non-descript activities were recorded. However, his father did describe some military operations that he was involved in or had direct knowledge of. One such entry described an unsuccessful operation in which a sixty-man team, apparently led by Roscoe, attempted to "take out" an airstrip in Taiwan.

Another entry described the assassination of a Chinese diplomat by an unidentified, smaller, more elite team. At the bottom of this page was the notation, "RE RIFLE." Ricky recalls reading other entries in the book where this same notation appeared at the bottom of the page. Later, Ricky would encounter this same "RE RIFLE" notation among additional artifacts left behind by his father.

While attending an artillery school at Fort Sill, Oklahoma in 1960, Roscoe wrote that he, *"met with an important man."* This *"important man"* was not identified by name, but Ricky told the authors that he may have met this *"important man"* at his father's funeral. Ricky recalls that after the ceremony, a man came up to him and introduced himself as "Colonel Carl Bond." The man did not make any comments about his father and only mentioned that he knew him, then walked away.

One ex-Marine commented to Gary Shaw that Roscoe's Fort Sill attendance may have been a "sheep-dipping" assignment. (*Note: In espionage, "sheep-dipping" refers to the "official," usually temporary, transfer of military personnel to non-military use for the purpose of covert action employment.)

U. S. Army
Artillery and Missile School
Fort Sill, Oklahoma

ARTILLERY BALLISTIC METEOROLOGY COURSE

Certificate of Proficiency

This certifies that

Cpl R. A. White

on 23 September 1960, completed satisfactorily the ARTILLERY BALLISTIC METEOROLOGY COURSE, Class Number 1-61, U. S. Army Artillery and Missile School in the following subcourses:

Visual Methods
RAWINS and Team Operation
Radiosonde Equipment and Techniques

Recorded as graduated:

MAJOR GENERAL, U. S. A.
COMMANDANT

COLONEL, ARTILLERY
SECRETARY

BRIGADIER GENERAL, U. S. A.
ASSISTANT COMMANDANT

*Certificate of Proficiency, Fort Sill, Oklahoma, September 23, 1960.*

## The Diary

Eventually, Ricky grew tired of reading the diary and put all the material back into the suitcase and did not revisit it until sometime in 1984.

Finally, with some free time on his hands, Ricky picked up the diary again and began reading. Ricky skipped through the pages to a time when his father was no longer in the Marines and stopped when he saw the entry for November 22, 1963. The words on these one-and-a-half pages quickly and completely captured his attention.

As he read, his first thought was that his father was playing some type of cruel joke. In disbelief, Ricky continued reading the words on these pages over and over. On these pages, his father documented in detail his direct involvement in the events in Dallas, Texas on November 22, 1963. Ricky told the authors, *"I read these pages so many times the words were burned into my brain."* (R. White, personal communication, April 28, 2018.)

There it was – his father's hand-written admission detailing his direct participation in the murder of President Kennedy. Ricky gave the book to Tricia. As she read the two pages, Ricky sat quietly and waited for her reaction.

Tricia told the authors that after having sat and read the entry so many times, she could almost recite it verbatim. During one visit to their home, the authors questioned Ricky and Tricia independently about the November 22 entry and what they remembered reading. The couple jointly provided the authors with their collective recollections regarding that important entry. This is what they remember reading:

> *"11-22-63—Lebanon (Sixth Floor), Saul (Records Bldg.), Mandarin (Stockade Fence). Shots fired from upper buildings for diversion. Shots fired, looks as if target was hit. Shot from fence, definite hit. Man on other side of fence in the way. Shots again from upper bldgs., no hit. Target open, fired, definite hit. Gun retrieved by man to the side, took to railcar area. Whirled over fence, took man down to protect myself. Ran around back of fence down*

> *embankment to car. Drove to Oak Cliff, met officer. Told officer not to drive by house. Something was at this point wrong. Forced to take out officer at 10th and Patton. Not going as planned. Back tracked to car, drove back to the area to take out other passenger. Failed to transport subject to Redbird [airport]. Realized what a mistake I had made, hope it is all over. Back to DPD awaiting information."*

The following are the authors' interpretations of the information contained in the one-and-one-half pages in Roscoe's diary for November 22, 1963.

**"*11-22-63*"**

The date of the assassination of President Kennedy in Dallas, Texas.

***"Lebanon (Sixth Floor), Saul (Records Bldg.), Mandarin (Stockade Fence)"***

The code names and corresponding shooting locations for Mandarin's, aka Roscoe White's, three-man assassination team. The identities of Lebanon and Saul are unknown.

(Note: Much was made of Roscoe's identification of "Saul" as one of the other assassins. Critics of Ricky's story vigorously declared that Ricky "stole" the name "Saul" from the book, *Appointment in Dallas,* by Hugh McDonald. The problem with this unfounded allegation was that Roscoe was dead and buried four years before the book's publication in 1975.)

***"Shots fired from upper buildings for diversion."***

According to Roscoe, to draw attention from firing positions *in front* of the limousine, "diversionary shots" were fired from upper floors of buildings located behind the motorcade. Evidence at the crime scene indicated that one bullet struck the grass near a manhole cover on the south side of Elm Street and was picked up by an unidentified man. Another shot bounced off the sidewalk on the north side of Elm while another shot struck the south curb on Main Street, ricocheted and slightly wounded a bystander.

***"Shots fired, looks as if target was hit.***

The origin of "shots [plural] fired" indicated that both shooters stationed in the buildings to the rear of the president fired at the same time and struck one or more of the limousine occupants. Either of these shots could have been the bullet that struck the president in the back – or the shot that hit Governor Connally.

***"Shot from fence, definite hit."***

Since Mandarin was the only shooter stationed in the stockade fence area, it indicated that he fired this shot. The president was hit in the throat from the front; consequently, there can be no doubt that this shot was fired from *in front* of the limousine.

***"Man on other side of fence in the way."***

Adjacent to Roscoe's position on the back side of the picket fence was a man – on the opposite side of the fence – who apparently was blocking Roscoe's view of the motorcade. This man prevented Roscoe from getting a clear shot at the president.

***"Shots again from upper bldgs., no hit."***

More shots from Lebanon and/or Saul that missed the target.

***"Target open, fired, definite hit."***

Apparently, the man who moments before was "in the way" no longer blocked Roscoe's field of vision; so, he shot. Apparently, Roscoe saw the results of this shot from his position behind the fence.

***"Gun retrieved by man to the side, took to railcar area."***

Roscoe passed his gun to an awaiting accomplice who escaped to the nearby railyard area.

Eyewitness Ed Hoffman said that he saw a man carrying a rifle running along the back side of the fence immediately after the shots. Hoffman watched as the man suddenly stopped and tossed the rifle to another man waiting near one of the railroad switch boxes. After breaking the rifle down into two pieces, this man placed the weapon into a soft bag and briskly walked north along the railroad tracks.

On February 23, 2008, with an American Sign language interpreter, Brian Edwards and Casey Quinlan met with Ed Hoffman and asked him to describe what he observed behind the picket fence just before the shooting. Ed recalled seeing a stocky man wearing a "dress hat" and a dark suit, walk around the east end of the picket fence to the back side (north side). This man walked towards a uniformed Dallas police officer who was standing by himself behind the fence. Ed remembered the officer was not wearing a hat and had dark hair. Ed said he could see the badge on the chest and shoulder patch on the uniform.

After standing near the policeman for a moment, the stocky man turned and walked around the east side of the fence and was no longer in view. Ed remembered the stocky man had a camera hanging from his neck.

Ed told Quinlan and Edwards that moments before the shooting, he saw a uniformed policeman walk around to the back side of the fence from the east and stand near a different man whom Ed had not previously seen. This policeman WAS wearing a hat and Ed did not know if this was the same officer he had seen moments before. After standing next to this man for a moment, the policeman walked around the fence at the east end and was no longer in view.

After the shooting, this second man turned and was now facing west towards Ed's location on Stemmons Freeway. The man was holding a rifle across his chest with both hands and was rapidly moving parallel to the fence in the direction of the railroad switch boxes. After a few seconds, the man stopped suddenly and tossed the rifle to another man who was wearing coveralls. Before the shooting, Ed had seen the man in the coveralls standing on the west side of one of the railroad switch boxes.

After catching the rifle, the man in the coveralls stood on the west side of the switch box and twisted the rifle into two separate pieces. The man then bent forward at the waist, placed both pieces of the rifle into a soft bag then quickly walked north along the railroad tracks and out of Ed's view.

***"Whirled over fence, took man down to protect myself."*** This suggested that Roscoe felt that he had to deal with someone who could identify him as being involved in the assassination. Was this the same man who moments before blocked Roscoe's view of the motorcade? To "protect himself," Roscoe "whirled over the fence" and took the man down. Exactly what this action entailed is unclear. Did he assault this man? Did he knock him to the ground? Did he shoot the man?

Interestingly, Jerry Coley, an employee of the *Dallas Morning News*, was in Dealey Plaza during the assassination. Immediately after the shots were fired, he ran toward the grassy knoll. (Note: Coley recalled the incident in a 2017 interview with Len Osanic.
See https://www.youtube.com/watch?v=hgqAm9jRpNU.)

*"Beside the corner of the picket fence, there at the top of those steps that go down the grassy knoll, I looked down at the top of those steps before you take the top step was a huge puddle that I thought was blood."* Sometime later, after he returned to the newspaper, Coley mentioned that he saw blood on the steps. Later, he and staff photographer Jim Hood returned to the exact location and noticed the now coagulated blood was clearly visible. Coley continued: "*Jim put his little finger on his right hand into that and stuck his tongue to it and said, 'Well, that's blood.'*" Hood took a photo of the spot and returned to the newspaper offices.

The following Monday, Coley and another reporter, Hugh Aynesworth, returned to the exact location in Dealey Plaza and discovered that the stain had been completely removed from the sidewalk. Author Shaw believes that reporter Aynesworth probably reported the incident to the FBI. Later that afternoon, two FBI agents arrived at the newspaper, contacted Hood and Coley, and demanded the negative and all the photo prints. Hood handed the print and the negative to the agents, who said: "*Boys, this conversation never took place, if you know what we mean.*"

Other witnesses in Dealey Plaza observed Roscoe White on the knoll immediately after the shooting.

Beverly Oliver watched the motorcade from the south side of Elm and immediately after the shots were fired, she observed two uniformed Dallas police officers standing near the east end of the picket fence. As cars from the motorcade were still traveling west on Elm, Beverly saw both officers walking diagonally down the knoll towards the street. She recognized one of the officers as "Geneva's husband" and noticed that he was not wearing a hat or gun belt. Beverly said "Geneva's husband" looked in her direction as he walked with the other officer. (Source: Oliver, Beverly. *Nightmare in Dallas*, 1994). (Note: Beverly worked at the Colony Club next door to Ruby's Carousel Club and was acquainted with Geneva who had worked for Ruby.)

Another witness was Dallas police motorcycle officer Robert "Bobby" Hargis. Hargis was riding on the left side of the presidential limousine as the shots were being fired. Hargis said that when a bullet hit Kennedy's head, blood and brain matter were thrown onto his face and uniform. He testified to the Warren Commission that he stopped, got off his motorcycle, ran to the north side of Elm Street, and looked in the direction of the triple underpass. (Source: 6H 152-153.)

Later, an assassination researcher interviewed Officer Hargis who stated that he encountered Roscoe on the knoll immediately after the shots were fired. Hargis said, *"Roscoe White was doing like I was...looking for someone who he (Roscoe) couldn't tell just like I couldn't tell where the shot was coming from."*

(https://www.youtube.com/watch?v=047rHDKqqxA&t=486s&pp=ygUeYm9iYnkgaGFyZ2lzIGpmayBhc3Nhc3NpbmF0aW9u).

*Jerry Coley in 2017*

***"Ran around back of fence down embankment to car."***

After dealing with the man on the south side of the picket fence, Roscoe turned and went back around the fence, crossed the parking lot and railroad tracks, and down an embankment to a "car." Did Roscoe drive his own car to the area or was he referring to another vehicle? Did he park a car there or was someone waiting for him? (Note: At the time of the assassination, Roscoe owned two vehicles; a white 1962 Ford Galaxie sedan and a dark Plymouth or Dodge.)

### *"Drove to Oak Cliff, met officer."*

Was this a chance encounter or a planned rendezvous between these two men? Was the "Officer" Tippit or another unidentified officer? Was this "officer" a co-conspirator or an unwitting participant? Tippit's movements and actions that afternoon seemed suspicious for several reasons:

(1) He was several miles from his assigned patrol district.
(2) At the time of the assassination he was sitting in his patrol car at the GLOCO gas station near the south entrance to the Houston Street viaduct watching cars coming out of downtown and across the Trinity River.
(3) He did not respond to calls from the police dispatcher.
(4) He placed a frantic phone call from inside the Top Ten Records store just before his death.
(5) He stopped a motorist named James Andrews who reported being pulled over by Tippit. Andrews said Tippit jumped out of the patrol car, ran up to his car, quickly looked into the back seat, and without saying a word, trotted back to the patrol car and sped away.

### *"Told officer not to drive by house."*

The housekeeper at 1026 North Beckley testified to the Warren Commission that she heard a car horn honk just as Oswald entered the residence at about 1 p.m. She looked out the front window and saw a Dallas police car with two occupants. After a few moments, the patrol car pulled away from the curb, made a right turn, and was out of her view.

Did Roscoe or Tippit already know Lee Oswald lived at this address? Why did Roscoe instruct the "Officer" (Tippit?) not to drive past the house? Were they supposed to pick up Oswald?

"***Something was at this point wrong.***"

Exactly what is wrong at this point is unclear but whatever it was, Roscoe believed he needed to take immediate action before it was too late.

***"Forced to take out officer at 10th and Patton.***"

The murder of Officer J. D. Tippit remains a mystery to researchers of the Kennedy assassination. Less than forty-five minutes after shots rang out in Dealey Plaza, gunfire erupted in the quiet neighborhood of Oak Cliff. A Dallas police officer was suddenly and violently gunned down and left lying in the street while the killer(s) fled the scene on foot. Later that evening, Lee Oswald was formally charged with Tippit's murder.

What transpired moments before Tippit was shot? Did Roscoe and Tippit get into an argument that escalated into a "kill or be killed" situation? Why did Roscoe believe it was necessary to kill Tippit? Roscoe's words seem clear: he drives to Oak Cliff and apparently meets Tippit, directs him not to drive by Oswald's rooming house, gets into some type of argument with Tippit, and is left with no alternative but to kill him to keep the plan from unraveling.

***"Not going as planned."***

After being "forced" to kill Tippit, whatever was "planned" was now falling apart and Roscoe was desperate to find a way out.

***"Back tracked to car, drove back to the area to take out other passenger."***

Roscoe gets back to a car, then returns to the area of 10th & Patton to search for the "other passenger" (Oswald?). Only one logical conclusion can be drawn from this statement – Roscoe was looking for Oswald – but purposely left Oswald's name out of the diary.

***"Failed to transport subject to Redbird."***

Roscoe never found Oswald and therefore, was not able to get him to Redbird Airport to facilitate his escape. Now, Oswald is on the loose and in danger of being captured by the police. If taken into custody, would Oswald talk about Roscoe's role in the plan?

Red Bird Airport, a small private facility located in what was then a somewhat remote area twelve miles south of downtown Dallas, has been a recurring subject in Kennedy assassination lore. Over the years, at different intervals and from different sources, information has surfaced suggesting that the airfield had been the scene of mysterious events. before and immediately after the assassination.

In 1974, Penn Jones and J. Gary Shaw were contacted by a man who told them that on the afternoon of the assassination, a private plane with engines running at full throttle was seized by Federal authorities at the airfield and placed under guard in a secure hangar for several days.

***"Realized what a mistake I had made, hope it is all over."*** Roscoe now realized the enormity of his deeds and understood that his participation in it was a terrible mistake.

***"Back to DPD awaiting information."***

Roscoe wrote that he returned to police headquarters. Did he go back to the station to await instructions or was he hoping to obtain information regarding the progress of the investigation? If he returned to the police station, as he wrote, then the events witnessed by Mike Robinson – as detailed by Walt Brown in *Treachery in Dallas* (1995) – are extremely important and validate a portion of Roscoe's activities that day.

**The Mike Robinson Story**

November 22, 1993, marked the thirtieth anniversary of the assassination and a large crowd was gathering in Dealey Plaza, but the police were moving everyone out of the area until the ceremony began. Veteran assassination researcher Dr. Walt Brown was part of the crowd that was pushed out of the plaza and onto the sidewalk in front of the Dal-Tex building. Brown was nearby when he saw a man being interviewed by a local television crew. After the interview was concluded, Brown introduced himself and asked if the man would be willing to retell his story. The following is a summary of that interview.

Mike Robinson was fourteen years old the day the president was killed. He and his friend, Glenn, whose father was Captain Frank Martin (who) had been with the DPD for thirty-three years and was in charge of the department's Juvenile Division, watched the motorcade as it passed by the police station at the intersection of Main and Harwood Streets.

After the motorcade passed their location, the two boys went to a theater and then learned the president had been shot. Assuming the police department would be the place to learn more about the shooting, Mike and Glenn ran back to police headquarters, checked in with Glenn's father on the third floor, and were present when Lee Oswald was brought to that floor. The boys stayed and watched as the third floor quickly filled with reporters and photographers.

*DPD Captain Frank Martin*

As early as 2:30 p.m., Mike said he heard numerous conversations by the police that declared Oswald was responsible for both crimes. Mike said this was when he first learned that Officer Tippit had been killed.

Mike said he and Glenn saw Oswald being taken to and from various offices on the third floor. They also witnessed motorcycle officer Bobby Hargis slam his helmet into a wall and subsequently had to be restrained by several of his fellow officers.

By the evening, the entire third floor was filled with police and the media, which made it impossible to walk down the hall. Mike saw Captain Martin and told him that he needed to use the restroom. Captain Martin took Mike to the lower level of the building where the officers had their lockers and pointed to the restroom.

Mike was completely alone when he entered the restroom. He entered one of the stalls and sat down. Just then, the silence was broken by three individuals in mid-conversation as they entered the restroom. Unsure whether he was supposed to be in the officer's facility, Mike lifted his feet and "hid" in the stall.

Initially, the men whispered, but eventually, one of the men raised his voice and used profanity. Mike recalled one of the men said, *"You knew you were supposed to kill Lee, then you stupid son of a bitch, you go kill a cop."* Then, another man entered the restroom and the first three men immediately stopped talking. The newest man to enter, whom Mike saw through the small gap between the side of the stall and the stall door, was wearing a blue police uniform. This man stood at the urinal, did his business, then left.

Mike heard one of the original three men state, *"Lee will have to be killed before they take him to Washington."*

Eventually, the three men left the restroom, but Mike stayed behind for several minutes before he exited the stall. As he passed through the police locker room, one officer, while changing out of his uniform, stared at Mike as if to say, *"Were you in there when we were?"*

In a follow-up interview with Robinson, Brown showed him photos of the officers on the Dallas police force at that time. Robinson picked out the photo of Roscoe White and commented that he was the officer who stared at him in the locker room.

On March 24, 1964, Robinson's friend's father, DPD Captain Frank Martin, was called to give testimony before Warren Commission junior counsel member Leon D. Hubert, Jr. The session took place at the United States Post Office in Dallas. The purpose of his testimony was related to the security in the basement of police headquarters when Oswald was shot.

Near the end of his testimony, Mr. Hubert asked if there was anything he would like to add to his testimony regarding the basement security. Martin replied, *"I – don't take this down."* Mr. Hubert cautioned him, *"Well, if you don't want to say it on the record, you'd better not say it at all."* Martin's response: *"There is a lot to be said, but probably be better if I don't say it."* On May 25, 1965, Captain Martin got sick on the job and died of apparent cancer on June 16, 1966. (Source: Jones, Penn, *Forgive My Grief*, Vol. II, page 16.)

(Full disclosure: some of the cited narratives with Robinson came to light via hypnosis conducted by an expert with a

Ph.D. in hypnotherapy. Brown wrote: "*Although to this day, when he* [Mike] *sees the photo of Roscoe White in the JFK Assassination Information Center (JFKAIC), he admits that it scares the hell out of him.*") (Source: Brown, W. (1995) *Treachery in Dallas,* Carroll & Graf, Inc.)

*Mike Robinson in 1967.*

Ricky also noted that in the last line of this diary entry, Roscoe explained how his other two team members gained access to the buildings overlooking Dealey Plaza. He wrote that Lebanon posed as a repairman for a heating and air conditioning company, and Saul posed as a building maintenance company employee.

As Ricky read these diary pages over and over, he became increasingly agitated and distraught. He recalled a conversation with family friend Phillip Jordan in 1978 when the House Select Committee on Assassinations (HSCA) reinvestigated President Kennedy's death.

**Phillip Jordan Speaks**

Phillip Dale Jordan grew up in Paris, Texas and attended the same high school as Ricky's mother. After Roscoe and Geneva were married, she introduced Jordan to her husband, and they quickly became friends. While Ricky was growing up, he recalls hearing rumors about Jordan; namely, that he was connected to the Mafia, was in military intelligence, and worked, or was still working for the Central Intelligence Agency. Ricky characterized Jordan as *"...a strange and scary guy."* (Source: R. White, personal communication, March 13, 2023.)

According to Ricky, during the last four years of his father's life, his family and the Jordans spent considerable time together socially. Ricky said that Jordan and his wife Twyla attended his father's funeral in 1971.

Ricky recalled a meeting with Jordan in 1978, when he and Tricia were living in Paris, Texas. One day as they were about to enter the local grocery store, they met Phillip Jordan and his wife Twyla. Standing outside the store, Jordan said that he needed to discuss an important matter with Ricky, specifically involving his father. Ricky and Tricia invited the Jordans to their home and while sitting in their living room, Jordan said Ricky's father was directly involved in the Kennedy assassination.

Jordan alerted Ricky that a government investigation was underway in Washington, D.C. (House Select Committee on Assassinations), and they were going to name his father as one of President Kennedy's assassins. Jordan said Ricky's father was selected to join a secret organization/unit while in the Marines. Ricky later recalled when Jordan said his father was one of the men who shot at President Kennedy; "he *was stating it as a fact."*

While Jordan talked, Ricky and Tricia remembered seeing bandages under his shirt. When they asked him about it, he said about one week before he met Ricky in the parking lot, two men broke into his house and shot him in the stomach. Jordan said he believed these men mistook him for Phillip E. Jordan, an agent with the Drug Enforcement Agency.

Jordan reiterated that he was sure the HSCA was going to name his father as a shooter. As they listened to Jordan, Ricky and Tricia said they were scared to ask too many questions, and they simply could not bring themselves to ask how Jordan learned all this information. Ricky said that during this first meeting, Jordan never said, *"Your mom told me this or your dad said that."* After about forty-five minutes, Jordan and his wife left.

Ricky and Tricia sat silently in the living room for a long time trying to process what Jordan told them. Later that evening, when Ricky went to work, Jordan's story weighed so heavily on his mind that he had trouble focusing on his work. Ricky said that everything Jordan described sounded as if it was from his knowledge as if it was fact.

The next evening, Ricky called Jordan and asked him to meet with them again. He agreed and invited them to his house. At that meeting, Jordan told them the whole story again, exactly as before. After the meeting, Ricky and Tricia went home and agreed that they would not discuss anything Jordan had told them with anyone – ever.

Ricky recalled that during the last four years of his father's life, the two families were very close and spent considerable time together socially. Ricky wondered if his father confided in Jordan and trusted him enough to keep the assassination material for him.

*Philip Jordan,*
*The Paris News,*
*November 21, 1962.*

The authors have been told by various sources, though unconfirmed, that Phillip Jordan was associated with the Dixie Mafia, a criminal organization whose group activities included the movement of stolen merchandise, illegal alcohol, and drugs.

On May 29, 1989, Ricky and his friend Andy Burke interviewed Phillip Jordan at his home in Paris, Texas. Jordan agreed to the interview but did not allow the interview to be recorded.

The following is a summary of that interview from Andy Burke's notes.

- He enlisted in the Navy in 1958 and became a nuclear arms instructor stationed at Lemoore, California.
- He was trained in New Mexico.

- He became involved with the CIA in 1960.
- He claimed that he was on the west coast of Cuba in April 1962 at the height of the Cuban missile crisis.
- Before he was discharged from the Navy in 1965, he was involved in an accident that severely burned his face. He spent time in a hospital with a naval guard outside his room at all times. This was when he realized that someone was out to get him.

In 1968, Jordan moved back to Paris, and in 1972, he started his own saddle-making business.

Jordan knew and briefly dated Geneva Toland (Roscoe's future wife) when they both were enrolled at Paris High School. He first met Roscoe in 1964 shortly after Geneva was treated at Sherman Veterans Hospital in Sherman, Texas. In 1968, Jordan said Roscoe gave him an envelope that contained photographs he collected while working on the Dallas police force. Jordan said he returned these photos to Geneva in late 1974 or early 1975.

Jordan said that while Roscoe lived in Dallas, he was heavily involved with the Freemasons, Roscoe's intelligence contacts were through the Dallas Naval Air Station and Jordan said that Roscoe had been working with the CIA since 1958. Additionally, he confirmed that Roscoe went through eight months of specialized training during his second tour of the Far East. After he [Roscoe] was discharged from the Marines, he continued working as an undercover agent for the government until the day he died.

Jordan said that in 1963, shortly after Roscoe left the military, he worked as an insurance agent for the American

National Life Insurance Company. His main contact with the government was through a woman named Hazel who worked at Jaggars-Chiles-Stovall, Incorporated. Sometime in August 1963, Roscoe was assigned a new contact named Jack Ruby, a man who worked with the government and the Mafia since the early 1950s.

Jordan said that when "Rock" started on the Dallas police force, he was assigned to the homicide bureau. This assignment afforded him full access to files regarding the investigation into the president's assassination but could also monitor the progress of the Tippit investigation.

Consequently, Roscoe learned the names and addresses of the witnesses who provided information contrary to the lone assassin scenario.

Jordan claims the three "backyard" photos of "Oswald" were doctored by Roscoe in the police department photo lab. He said that Roscoe took the altered photos to Ruth Paine's home and planted them for the police to find later. After the assassination, Roscoe learned that only two of the photos were recovered. Subsequently, Roscoe returned to Paine's home, retrieved the third photo, and in the presence of Marina Oswald, burned the negative in Paine's bathroom. (Note: This third photo, the only one of the three that was made from its original negative, Commission Exhibit 133 C, was later found among Roscoe's assassination-related materials.)

Jordan said Roscoe knew of Oswald's involvement, and that later, he [Oswald] was set up by the government. Ruby was ordered to kill Oswald because those involved in the plot feared he would talk about the Mafia's role in the assassination. After Ruby shot Oswald, the government got Roscoe out of Dallas until "they" were sure that Ruby would not talk. Later, Roscoe was brought back to Dallas and continued working in the police department for another two years. During this continued employment, Roscoe was involved in the witness elimination program.

After Roscoe left the police force, the family moved to Arkansas where "Rock" continued to work for the government. (Note: Jordan never identified what Roscoe did in Arkansas.)

Ricky contacted Jordan again with hopes of learning more about his father, particularly as related to the November 1963 events. At this meeting, Jordan informed Ricky that his father – readily known by his codename "Mandarin" – was the leader of one of the assassination teams ordered to kill President Kennedy. (Note: Additional corroboration of these orders is discussed in Chapters Five and Six.)

Phillip Jordan died in 1996 at the age of 56.

Upset by what he read in the diary, Ricky confronted his mother and insisted that she read Roscoe's November 22 entries. When Geneva finished, Ricky, full of frustration, asked whether she knew about this. Before Geneva had time to respond, Ricky – overcome with emotion that bordered on rage – demanded, *"Why have you never told me about this?"* After a long pause, Geneva held up the diary and said, *"Well, not about this, but I always knew he had something to do with it. I figured he put it down in writing somewhere.*

Ricky remembers the look on his mother's face conveyed a combination of resignation, despondency, and fear. She started crying and told Ricky that she was sorry for not confiding in him. Realizing his suspicions were true, Ricky broke down and began to cry. He told the authors that he, *"...bawled like a baby and we hugged each other and had a good, long cry.* (Source: R. White, personal communication, February 7, 2023).

There it was, corroboration from multiple sources: Phillip Jordan, his mother, and a handwritten admission from his father. Ricky now realized his world would never be the same.

Ricky telephoned his brother Tony in Lubbock, Texas, and without elaborating, told him of discovering something very disturbing about the Kennedy assassination in their father's diary. Ricky wanted his brother to come to Midland right away to discuss the matter. Tony was ambivalent and said he would see the diary later.

On Christmas Eve 1987, Tony and his family were traveling from Lubbock to Ricky's home in Midland to celebrate the holiday with his brother and mother. About two hours into the trip, Tony encountered a driving snowstorm and had to return to Lubbock. Consequently, Tony would never see the diary.

Ricky was so protective of the diary that he did not allow anyone outside the family to see or read it. However, neither

Ricky nor Tricia knew that their friend and babysitter Denise Carter had read a portion of the diary while she was in their home. In 1992, Ms. Carter briefly appeared in the seven-part investigative report entitled *The West Texas Connection* that aired on KMID-TV, a Midland, Texas television station.

During the interview, Ms. Carter freely admitted that she read a portion of the diary when Ricky and Tricia were at work.

In an interview with the authors, Ms. Carter said she picked up the book, flipped through the pages, and read some of the entries. She described the book as *"about the size of a little legal pad with a black cover and about an inch thick."* She recalled seeing names and numbers but was not familiar with their meanings. Realizing she was probably not supposed to be reading the book, she returned it to its original position on the pool table. On another occasion, while Ricky and Tricia were at work, she showed the book to her husband who dismissed the writing as nonsense. (Source: D. Carter, personal communications, February 9, 2023.)

Denise said she was present when FBI agents Tom Farris and Ron Butler arrived at the White's home demanding to speak to Ricky. Denise told the agents that Ricky was at work. Immediately, the agents "ordered" her to call him and have him return home at once.

When Ricky arrived home, one of the agents directed him to transfer all of his father's material into a box. Denise said she helped Ricky place the material into the box, including the diary. She watched as Ricky carried the box to his car and put it in the trunk. Then, as instructed Ricky drove away directly behind the agents.

Other witnesses saw the diary and confirmed its existence. On one occasion, for no known reason, Ricky took the diary to work in his briefcase. His supervisor opened Ricky's briefcase, picked up the diary, and briefly scanned its pages before returning it to the briefcase. (Source: R. White, personal communication, March 13, 2023).

David Gachot, a co-worker of Roscoe's and one of his pallbearers, told Ricky he remembered seeing his father writing in a book during coffee and lunch breaks. He said Roscoe kept the book in his toolbox. (Source: Audio interview of David Gachot by Andy Burke, 1989.)

Looking back on the early years of his life, Ricky recalled some of the strange and memorable experiences with his father.

He recalled the following:

- Shortly before the Kennedy assassination, his father began working for the Dallas Police Department. Initially, Ricky had not considered this to be unusual; but now, he wondered if it was part of a sophisticated plan. At about this same time, his mother was working part-time at Jack Ruby's Carousel Club.
- Jack Ruby, the killer of the alleged assassin, visited their home on several occasions.
- His father suddenly returned to the house shortly after Ruby shot Oswald. Roscoe's sudden appearance interrupted Ricky's third birthday party

and the family was hastily taken to Geneva's parents' home in Paris, Texas.

- His father's disappearance for several days after leaving them in Paris.
- A mysterious encampment at Vidor, Texas.
- A long night-time trip to the docks in New Orleans.
- Fishing at Lake Whitney with his father who, with tears in his eyes, solemnly told him, *"Son, sometimes you do things you think are right at the time but later realize they're not."*
- His father's horrible injury at his place of employment.
- His mother possessed many official Dallas police crime photographs.
- Investigators from Senator Schweiker's Committee visited their home in 1976.
- Phillip Jordan's cryptic message in 1978: *"It's all going to come out now, and you need to know, before it appears in the news, that your dad was involved in the killing of President Kennedy."*
- Investigators from the House Select Committee on Assassinations visited their home in 1978. The investigators asked about "microdots" and confiscated all his father's assassination-related materials. Ricky wondered: *"Was the government – as Philip Jordan claimed – looking at this father as being involved in the assassination?"*
- The trips to the "hunting" lodge in Van Horn, Texas where he watched his father and other men shooting at targets.

The discovery of the diary motivated Ricky to seek more information about his father and his suspected involvement in the JFK assassination.

One recollection that always concerned him was his father's "hunting" trips to far west Texas mentioned above.

**Van Horn, Texas: A Training Site?**

Ricky recalled that as a young boy, he made two "hunting" trips with his father to Van Horn, Texas located in west Texas. Ricky also remembered that on one trip he met and played with other children of the same age. He remembered staying at a small cabin that had been built into the side of a mountain. (Source: Ricky White, personal communication, April 28, 2018.)

On the second day of one trip, Ricky remembers hearing gunshots from the canyon. Ricky and some of the other children crawled to the top of a bluff where they saw his father and the other men shooting at targets at the edge of the ravine. He remembered the men shooting at mannequins. However, Ricky admitted that he might be "jumbling up" that memory with a movie segment he saw in the 1973 movie *Executive Action*; the movie depicted scenes similar to what he remembered from the trip. (Source: Ricky White, personal communication, April 28, 2018.)

In 1990, Ricky provided J. Gary Shaw with a copy of a Van Horn postcard postmarked March 1961 that Roscoe had sent to his mother and stepfather. The card had a postal stamp from Sierra Blanca, Texas located a few miles west of Van Horn. Later, after learning about his father's "secret" life, Ricky believed his father went to Van Horn to train with the other men for the Dealey Plaza ambush.

On July 3, 1990, Gary Shaw received a phone call from Ricky White who was in Van Horn. Ricky stated that he had found the cabin located in a very remote area of the nearby Beach Mountains, located about two miles northwest of Van Horn. Locals referred to the area as the "Old Beach Headquarters." Later, Shaw learned that in the 1950s, the military held maneuvers near this location and that it once had a runway for small aircraft.

It is interesting, if not intriguing, that one of the Navy Intelligence officers involved with the CIA in some of their early sixties assassination operations was reported to have *"...owned land in far west Texas by a guns-for-drugs landing strip."* (Emphasis added.) (Source: Brewton, Pete; *The Mafia, CIA & George Bush*, p. xxv).

Van Horn is in West Texas just east of El Paso, Texas. Records showed that in May 1962, this same naval intelligence officer, while stationed at Guantanamo Bay, Cuba, flew out of El Paso to Miami for a meeting with a top CIA agent involved in the CIA's ZRRIFLE assassination program. (Source: NARA Record No. 104-10163-10206) The closest major airport to Van Horn is in El Paso.

In a segment for the May 1993 Midland/Odessa's KMID-TV expose on the Roscoe White story, reporter Mike Gibson traveled to Van Horn, Texas, and located the same isolated cabin that Ricky described. Gibson brought along Eddie Owen, a radio technician and former member of the Texas National Guard. While searching one of the outbuildings behind the cabin, Gibson and Owens discovered a large collection of radio equipment and a large directional antenna on the property.

Later in the segment, Gibson interviewed retired Air Force Colonel Glover Bruce Brock, who served as Chief of Communications for the National Security Agency for thirty-one years. Brock was responsible for intercepting radio messages from around the world. At some point in the past, Colonel Brock also operated the largest cryptographic communications in the world from Washington, D.C.

Brock was shown film of the radio equipment and identified it as having been manufactured by a company based in Kansas City (Note: Brock was referring to the King Radio Corporation, an avionics company founded in Kansas City, Missouri by Ed King. In 1948, King Radio began manufacturing components for Collins Radio.

According to Brock, the equipment was built before World War II primarily for export to South American countries. His first reaction was:

> *"When I first saw it, I knew it was for an illegal operation I'm sure out there in Van Horn...what else was it for? There was nothing legal going on out there that would need that type of communication. Now that antenna is pointed towards Mexico City... it's a directional type antenna and I have books that have that same type of antenna."*

In June 1993, JFKAIC, co-director Larry Howard traveled to the Van Horn site where he discovered a small box containing approximately 2,000 empty 6.5mm rifle casings inside a room attached to the cabin.

Significant to Howard's discovery is the fact that in 1963, 6.5mm ammunition was uncommon in the United States. Oswald's alleged ammunition came from a batch of four million rounds manufactured in 1954 by Western Cartridge Company. The shells found at the Texas School Book Depository were allegedly made under government contract DA-23-296-ORD-27 <u>for the United States Marine Corps</u> (emphasis ours). A high-ranking FBI criminalist said that this type of ammunition does not fit and cannot be fired in any of the USMC weapons which *"... gives rise to the obvious speculation that it is a contract for ammunition placed by CIA with Western under a USMC cover for concealment purposes."* (Melanson, Phillip H. *Spy Saga: Lee Harvey Oswald and U.S. Intelligence*, p. 113)

Gary learned that in 1963, the property was owned by a man named George Walker and was part of the Yates Estate. George Walker was a prominent attorney in Van Horn and at one time leased the site to a man whose last name was "Bowers." According to Walker, Bowers said the property would be used during deer hunting season, however, Walker did not recall anyone being at the property during deer season. (Note: As will be seen in the next chapter, the name "C. Bowers" appears on each of the three "Navy Int." cables sent to "Mandarin.")

*Beach Mountain*

*Video capture of Gibson and Owens*
*approaching the cabin near*
*Van Horn, Texas.*

*Video capture showing vintage radio equipment found at the cabin.*

*Video capture of the directional antenna and cabin in the background.*

**The Dallas Police SECRET Memo**

As noted in Chapter 3, the existence of the Roscoe White diary was authenticated in the January 26, 1988 memo from DPD Corporal Jack Beavers of the Intelligence Unit to Captain W. R. Rollins. This memo stated that he (Beavers) was contacted by Luckie on January 26, 1988, and was told that *"...the FBI had taken over the investigation."* Most importantly, Beavers wrote that Luckie told him, ***"...the FBI had met with Ricky White, had seen the photos and diary..."*** Notice in this statement that Luckie admitted that the FBI saw the diary that they claimed didn't even exist.

**The FBI: Tampering with the Evidence?**

In addition to the problems mentioned earlier concerning the Oswald diary, there are also examples of FBI skullduggery regarding some of Oswald's other writings. One such example relates to a "blue memo book" that was found and turned over to the FBI by Secret Service Agent Mike Howard. According to Howard, this memo book *"... contained notations by Oswald"* saying that *"... he intended to kill General Edwin A. Walker, Governor John Connally, and Vice President Lyndon Johnson and directly underneath the reference to Connally, Oswald had drawn a dagger with blood dripping from it."*

Before the book reached the Warren Commission this page had been removed. This bit of evidence tampering was not publicly known until about 30 years after the assassination; and, no surprise, the removed pages remain missing to this day. (Source: Cochran, Mike, Associated Press writer; *Cleburne Times-Review*, 11/18/93, p. 6A. Also, Meek, Jeffrey L., *The JFK Files: Pieces of the Puzzle, pp. 218-222)*

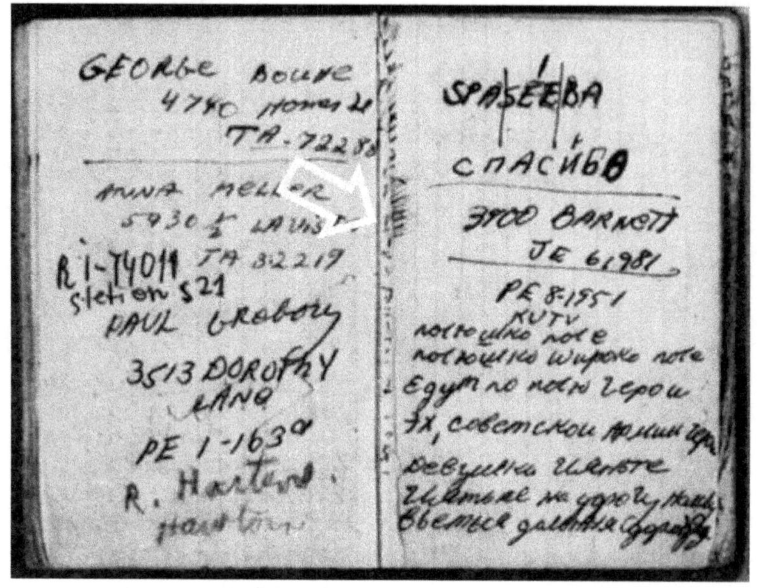


*Oswald's blue memo book with missing pages.*

On another occasion, ten days before the assassination, Oswald hand-delivered a message to an agent at the Dallas FBI Field Office. After Ruby shot and killed Oswald, the Dallas Special Agent in Charge, J. Gordon Shanklin, ordered the message destroyed and it was flushed down the toilet by Special Agent James Hosty. Once again, this official destruction of potentially important evidence only became publicly known about twelve years after the assassination.

Considering this and other examples of FBI subterfuge, as well as several other detestable actions and inactions regarding the agency's investigation into President Kennedy's death, who do you believe?

It is clear that this nation's chief investigative agency had no qualms about destroying or concealing troublesome evidence — and unhesitatingly did so. **Any** evidence that posed a problem to the government's lone gunman myth would never see the light of day. Accordingly, the stolen Roscoe White diary quickly joined the ranks of the disappearing Oswald "blue memo book" page and the destroyed Oswald message.

Ricky and Tricia are one hundred percent convinced that Roscoe's revealing diary was taken during the disconcerting and unannounced visit to their home by FBI SA Thomas Farris.

Of course, the Bureau, in deceitful fashion, *"categorically denied"* the couple's accusation.

Co-authors Shaw and Edwards believe Ricky and Tricia.

# CHAPTER FIVE:
## Orders for "Mandarin" aka Roscoe White

In actions and subtle comments before his death, Roscoe White hinted at the existence of materials that could one day be of great significance and value.

Ricky White, his brother Tony, and their mother Geneva, vividly recall the day at the family's weekend cabin at Lake Whitney, Texas, when Roscoe spent several hours digging a deep hole with a pick and shovel in the back of the house. Ricky distinctly remembers watching his father bury a "metal box" in that hole.

On June 8, 1990, Ricky, J. Gary Shaw, Larry Howard, and Joe West traveled to the cabin at Lake Whitney, Texas. Using picks and shovels, the four men dug several large holes around the property but found nothing. Not to be deterred, it was arranged for a backhoe to be brought to the property the next day. The backhoe operator was directed to dig on the northwest side

*Gary Shaw and Joe West watch as Ricky digs along the foundation of the Lake Whitney cabin.*

of the cabin. A twelve-foot by twelve-foot by two-foot-deep hole was dug but again nothing was found. They returned to Cleburne, Texas, and stayed at the home of J. Gary Shaw. It was assumed that Roscoe had either destroyed or re-hidden the "metal box" before the family sold the cabin about a year before his death.

After leaving Lake Whitney, Ricky drove to his grandparents' former home in Paris, Texas, and searched the abandoned home. There, in the attic, Ricky discovered a dusty, sealed, water-tight metal canister. (Note: This is the house where Roscoe's footlocker was found in 1982.)

*Ricky found this metal canister in the attic of his grandparents' home. Courtesy of Ricky White.*

Tossing the canister in the car, Ricky drove home to Midland. The following morning Ricky and Tricia were able to open the tightly sealed waterproof canister utilizing a crowbar and strap. The contents of the canister shocked the couple. Found inside were:

– One of Roscoe's dog tags and neck chain.
– Three typed cable messages sandwiched and sealed between two sheets of plastic that had yellowed with age. These were addressed to Roscoe's codename, "Mandarin," and included his military serial number.
– A shorthand textbook that had been crudely converted into a scrapbook with pasted-in newspaper clippings about the Kennedy assassination.
– Many of the book's pages contained hand-scribbled pencil notations, numbers, and other markings. Among these, many were indecipherable while others appeared to have been written in some type of code.
– In a second set of sealed plastic sheets there were several assassination-related newspaper clippings, including one of Jack Ruby, and several White family photo negatives that included images of Roscoe's parents

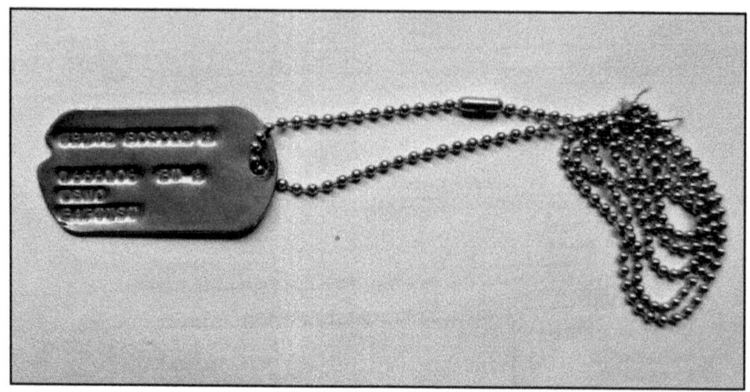

*Roscoe White's dog tag and chain.*
*Courtesy of Ricky White.*

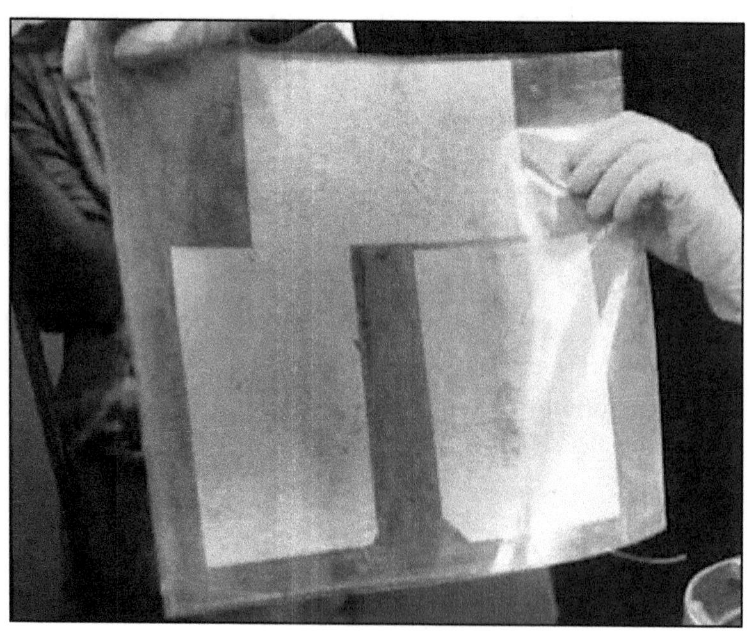

*Cables for Mandarin.*
*Photo by J. Gary Shaw*

*Textbook used for Roscoe's scrapbook.*

*Dallas Times Herald newspaper clippings*
*Top clipping: April 1, 1966*
*Bottom clipping: September 24, 1964*

*(top right) J. W. Harrington, Roscoe's maternal grandfather.*

*(center left) Lida "Merle" Rogers (White), Roscoe's mother*

*(bottom right) Roscoe's Aunt Agnes (middle), unknown woman (left)*

Undoubtedly, Roscoe's dog tag and the images of his mother and grandfather left no doubt who the owner of the canister was. The "scrapbook" also bore Roscoe's name, military serial number, and handwritten signature, further pointing to Roscoe as the scrapbook's creator and owner.

The focus of this chapter will be the three cable messages — their sender, recipient, content, and validity. The unusual "scrapbook" will be covered in another chapter.

**Cables to Mandarin:**

**THE SENDER: "NAVY INT."**

All headings for the three messages have the same basic six-line format beginning with "**Navy Int.**" Below this it reads "**Code A MRC**" followed by the words "**Remark data"** and Roscoe's military serial number, "**1666106**."

Below are these four lines of initials which appear to be references to three U.S. military acronyms: "**NRC", "VDC" and "NAC**."

The last line in the heading denotes the date of each message: "**Feb. 63**", "**Sept. 63,**" and "**Dec. 63**."

**THE RECIPIENT: "MANDARIN" — Roscoe A. White**

All three messages are addressed to "**Remarks Mandarin**." (Note: Ricky remembers reading in the missing diary that "Mandarin" was his father's code name.)

The first two messages are designated as “**Code A,**” and the last message had the heading “**Code C**.” The meaning of these designations is unknown.

As to the four acronyms in the heading, Gary Shaw interviewed a former Marine who knew both Roscoe White and Lee Oswald and was familiar with military acronyms of that time. He said that the initials on the cables referred to the following:

**“MRC”** – Marine Reserve Center
**“NRC”** – Navy Reserve Center
**“VDC”** – Aviation Reserve Center
**“NAC”** – Naval Air Center

The relationship of these acronyms to the messages is not known.

## ASSIGNMENT LEADER: “C. BOWERS”

All three messages are signed off by “C. Bowers,” followed by the acronym, “**OSHA**.” The identity of “**C. Bowers**” is unknown at this time but the authors are hoping that after publication of this book, someone will come forward with his identity.

The same former Marine mentioned above has reported that the acronym “**OSHA**” is a reference to the “Office of Special Handling Assignments.”

Typed at the very bottom of each message is: “**RE-rifle Code AAA Destroy /on/**.”

The meaning of "**Code AAA Destroy /on/**" in the concluding line of all three messages is not known. It may simply have been an order that the messages be destroyed; an order Roscoe, for reasons known only to himself, obviously ignored.

However, "**RE-rifle**" appears to be a military or intelligence agency cryptonym similar to the CIA cryptonym ZR/RIFLE, a program that included "executive action," i.e., "assassination." This program was a covert operation not publicly revealed until the mid-1970s, several years <u>after</u> Roscoe White died.

## THE CABLE'S CONTENT - MANDARIN'S ASSIGNMENTS

The following is an analysis of Roscoe's orders as contained in the three cable messages with our best effort at interpretation and explanation.

## CABLE # 1

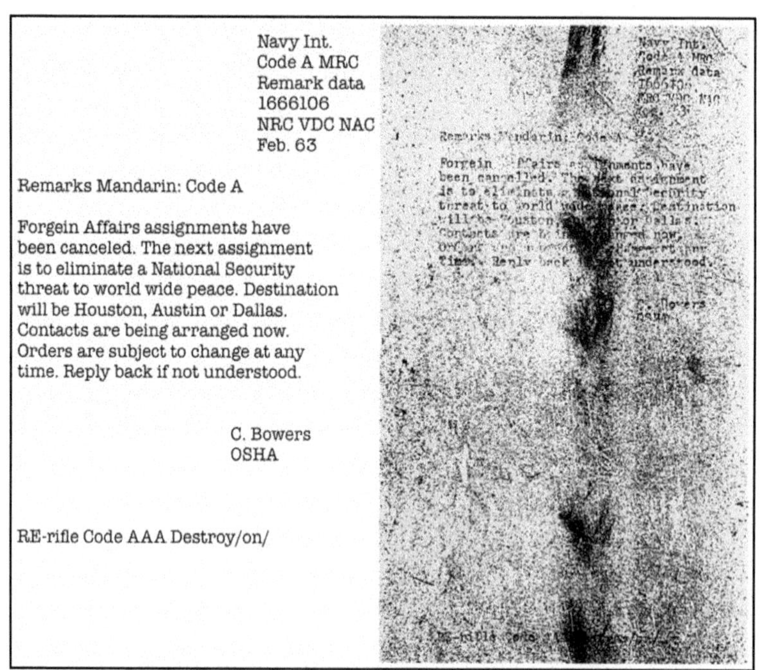

Navy Int.
Code A MRC
Remark data
1666106
NRC VDC NAC
Feb. 63

Remarks Mandarin: Code A

Forgein Affairs assignments have been canceled. The next assignment is to eliminate a National Security threat to world wide peace. Destination will be Houston, Austin or Dallas. Contacts are being arranged now. Orders are subject to change at any time. Reply back if not understood.

C. Bowers
OSHA

RE-rifle Code AAA Destroy/on/

*Original Cable #1 and transcription*

### "Feb. 63."

The February 1963 cable was the same month Roscoe received his honorable discharge.

In December 1962, while still in the Marines, he submitted his application to the Dallas Police Department.

***"Forgein*** [sic] ***Affairs assignments have been canceled."***
Whatever assignments Mandarin had outside of the continental United States were now rescinded. What these may have involved is unknown; but according to Roscoe's deathbed confession, these assignments included *"taking lives on both foreign and domestic soil."*

***"The next assignment is to eliminate a National Security threat to world wide peace."***
Roscoe's new assignment was domestic, one that involved the elimination, i.e., the removal (assassination) of someone (the "Target") who his superiors considered to be an imminent threat to U.S. security and world peace.

***"Destination will be Houston, Austin or Dallas."***
Roscoe's superiors had pre-selected three Texas cities as potential "elimination" sites.

***"Contacts are being arranged now."***
Roscoe's operational team was being selected and moved into position.

***"Orders are subject to change at any time."***
Roscoe's orders had to be flexible in the event of possible changes in the "Target's" travel itinerary, etc.

***"Reply back if not understood."***
Roscoe was to contact his leader immediately if he did not fully understand this new assignment.

## CABLE #2:

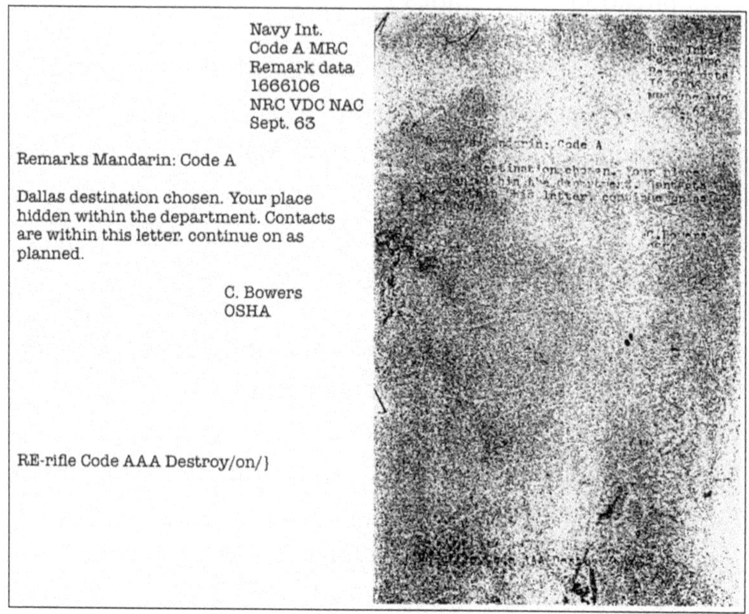

Navy Int.
Code A MRC
Remark data
1666106
NRC VDC NAC
Sept. 63

Remarks Mandarin: Code A

Dallas destination chosen. Your place hidden within the department. Contacts are within this letter. continue on as planned.

C. Bowers
OSHA

RE-rifle Code AAA Destroy/on/}

*Original Cable #2 and transcription*

### "Sept. 63."

In September 1963, Roscoe was working weekends at Roadway Express Company in Dallas. His Dallas Police Department pre-employment background investigation had been completed and forwarded to Chief Jesse Curry for final approval. Roscoe had also made arrangements for Geneva to go to work as a hostess for Jack Ruby.

### *"Dallas destination chosen."*

Roscoe is informed that the city of Dallas has been selected as the location for the elimination of the perceived "threat."

***"Your place hidden within the department."***

Although Roscoe submitted his application for employment with the Dallas Police Department in December 1962, he was not officially hired until October 1963, one month after this September 1963 cable. Both he and his superiors must have known that his hiring was a foregone conclusion, and his cover ("hidden") was complete.

***"Contacts are within this letter."***

This statement is somewhat puzzling. Does *"Contacts are within this letter"* mean that the cable was delivered with an accompanying letter listing these "Contacts?" Or does it mean that there is a coded message hidden within the body of the cable?

***"continue on as planned."***

This statement directs Roscoe to proceed with his assignment just as it had already been laid out.

## CABLE # 3:

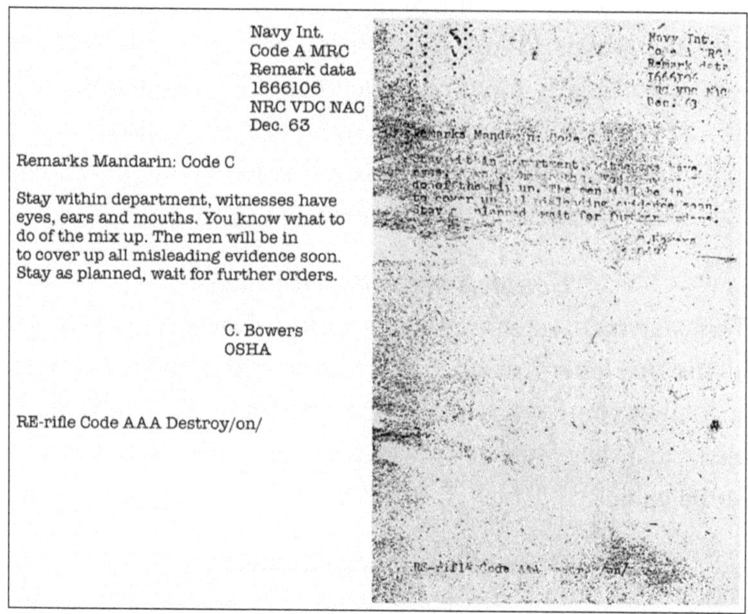

Navy Int.
Code A MRC
Remark data
1666106
NRC VDC NAC
Dec. 63

Remarks Mandarin: Code C

Stay within department, witnesses have eyes, ears and mouths. You know what to do of the mix up. The men will be in to cover up all misleading evidence soon. Stay as planned, wait for further orders.

C. Bowers
OSHA

RE-rifle Code AAA Destroy/on/

*Original Cable #3 and transcript*

**"Dec. 63."**

This is the month following the events of November 22-24, 1963, when Roscoe began his recruit training with the Dallas Police Academy. He is now in a position to carry out his next assignment which was:

***"Stay within department, witnesses have eyes, ears and mouths."***

Here Roscoe was ordered to stay with the Dallas Police. His job now was to observe what was transpiring with the investigation and with the various witnesses to the events of that tragic weekend.

***"You know what to do of the mix up."***

It appears that Roscoe had already been made aware of the potential for problems with such an assignment and had been already briefed as to what he was expected to do about them.

***"The men will be in to cover up all misleading evidence soon."***

Roscoe is advised that he's not alone in the follow-up (mop-up) aspects of his assignment and help is on its way. Additionally, evidence pointing toward Oswald as a lone assassin will be put into place and any and all contrary ("misleading") evidence will be removed and/or covered up.

***"Stay as planned, wait for further orders."***

Again, Roscoe is instructed that he is to remain with the police department as planned until he receives new or additional orders.

## "NAVY INT."

Who/what is "Navy Int."? — the source and authority behind the cables?

It's important to note here that the Marine Corps, though an independent branch of the United States military, is <u>under</u> the jurisdiction of the Department of the Navy. As such, the Marine Corps also falls under the auspices of the Office of Naval Intelligence, ONI or, to some, simply Navy Intelligence.

Is there a possible link between the Roscoe White cables and Navy Intelligence? Actually, there is, and it involves several intriguing and somewhat connecting incidents and individuals.

The record indicates that the ONI was quickly involved in the assassination investigation. However, when the JFK Assassination Records Review Board (AARB) attempted to gather all assassination-related files, they described the ONI, *"as a puzzle, if not a black hole."* (Lardner, G. Jr, *Washington Post*, Sept. 29, 1998, p. A15.)

**The ONI and Assassination**

On his informative blog JFKCountercoup, writer/researcher Bill Kelly wrote:

*"We do know that* ***the ONI played a major role in the study of assassination*** *and various ways, means, and methods to accomplish it." At a NATO conference in Norway... U. S. Navy Lt. Commander Thomas Narut was quoted in the London Sunday Times as saying that "...such research is continuous, ongoing and operational." According to the Narut "... combat readiness units... include men for commando-type operations and... for insertion into US embassies undercover...ready to kill in those countries should the need arise."* (Emphasis ours)

One such example of ONI involvement in assassinations is found in the revealing book, *Deadly Secrets* by William Turner and Warren Hinckle, who wrote:

> *"After the American Embassy in Havana was closed in January 1961, the sprawling Guantánamo Naval*

> *base became doubly important as an intelligence post and clandestine staging area. The CIA collaborated closely with its naval hosts, but on this assassination plot ONI appears to have been in the driver's seat. The officer in charge was a Navy lieutenant commander, and one of the assassins had long been under ONI control."* (emphasis added) (p. 114)

The Navy Lieutenant Commander was Jack Modesett, and the ONI assassin was Luis Balbuena. In a February 1962 letter, Balbuena wrote and asked his cousin to: *"... obtain by all the means possible two sniper rifles with telescopic sights, two Thompson sub-machine guns ...and six 45-caliber pistols."* He requested they be sent parcel post *"... as if they were replacement parts..."* to Lt. J. G. Jack Modesett at a Navy Fleet address in New York. No problem, nothing sinister here.

In May of 1962, Navy Lieutenant Commander John H. "Jack" Modesett, Jr. was stationed at Guantanamo (Cuba) Naval Base as an assistant to Harold "Hal" Feeney, the base's intelligence Officer (Office of Naval Intelligence, ONI).

Interestingly, Jack Modesett, Jr's., father, John H. "Jack" Modesett, Sr., was a Corpus Christi, Texas oilman, and a partner with President Kennedy's father, Joseph P. Kennedy in Mokeen Oil Company.

On April 14, 1962, Modesett, Sr. was killed in a one-car accident. Records show that on the same day his father was killed, his son, Jack, Jr. flew to Miami, the location of the

CIA's JMWAVE station. Records also show that top CIA agents William Harvey and James O'Connell, along with Harvey's "good friend" and Mafia hitman John Roselli, were meeting in Miami that same day. Was this a coincidence?

Harvey is well known as the leader in the CIA's notorious ZRRIFLE "executive action" assassination program. He also passionately hated President Kennedy and his brother, Robert. Harvey's top man was CIA agent David A. Morales, a man who confessed to his friends that, *"We got that SOB Kennedy."*

*David A. Morales* *John "Jack" Modesett, Jr.*

On May 11, 1962, about a month after Modesett's visit to JMWAVE, he flew from El Paso, Texas to Miami where he contacted David Morales at JMWAVE. One week later, on May 18, 1962, Morales wrote a three-page

"MEMORANDUM OF CONTACT," in which he was highly complementary of Modesett's demeanor and abilities and writes that the two men had made arrangements; *"...to keep in touch with each other by mail on problems of mutual interest."* (emphasis added). This seems to tie the ONI with the CIA and their ZRRIFLE assassination program.

**A Very Suspicious ONI Special Agent**

Another ONI connection includes an important character named John Mason Lankford of Fort Worth, Texas. Writer/researcher Bill Kelly has written about this man in his blog JFKCountercoup. Kelly says at the time of the assassination, Lankford was a Special Agent for the Office of Naval Intelligence (ONI), often referred to as the Navy Intelligence Service (NIS). Navy Intelligence Service, or NIS, was commonly used to refer to ONI. In fact, an associate of Lankford's in the ONI Fort Worth office, Arthur C. Sullivan used the "NIS" designation rather than "ONI" on his cemetery headstone.

*John Mason Lankford*

Lankford was an “old acquaintance” of Secret Service Agent Mike Howard. It was Agent Howard who called on Lankford, who at the time was also Fort Worth’s Fire Marshal, to assist him with the security of the president while he was staying in Fort Worth’s Texas Hotel on the night before his assassination. This was also the night and morning that several of JFK’s Secret Service security team decided to abdicate their responsibilities and party into the early morning hours at a nearby notorious night spot, The Cellar. The Cellar, owned by Pat Kirkwood, one of Jack Ruby’s pals, repeatedly employed some of Ruby’s strippers, including Little Lynn.

On the Sunday morning following the assassination, Agent Howard once again called on Lankford to assist him with security for alleged assassin Oswald's wife, Marina, her two children, and his mother.

Another connection is that one of Lankford's informants at the time was former Navy man Robert Kermit Patterson, who had been furnishing information to Lankford for some time. Four days after the assassination, Lankford reported to the FBI that Patterson told him that he had seen Ruby and Oswald together.

What does all this have to do with Roscoe White and the mysterious cables? From 1948 to 1972, John Lankford of Navy Intelligence served as Director of Security for either General Dynamics or its Convair Division. Roscoe White worked at Convair from May 8, 1956, to July 28, 1956, and as Director of Security, Lankford provided verification of White's brief employment for his 1962 Dallas Police Department employment application.

Subject: Roscoe Anthony White, Police Applicant — page 2

EMPLOYMENT

Mr. D. B. Rogers, 214 NE 28th Street, Paris, Texas. Applicant's stepfather stated:

"We moved to Paris in 1953. Rock stayed in Arkansas with his grandfather until he finished high school in 1954. He lived with us and worked for me at the saw mill until he went into the service in 1957. He did go to Fort Worth for about three months in 1956 and worked for Corvair. He was a hard worker and never did give me any trouble."

The applicant was employed by Corvair Corporation, Fort Worth, Texas, May 8, 1956 and quit for other employment on July, 28, 1956. He is eligible for rehire.

(Above information from Mr. J. M. Langford, Security Division, Corvair. The applicant did not list this employment on personal history statement.)

*Page 2 of pre-employment investigation of Roscoe White.*

For reasons unknown, Roscoe failed to mention his brief employment with Convair on his police application. The police investigator only learned of this after speaking with Roscoe's stepfather, Daniel Boone Rogers.

Lankford reported directly to the Director of Navy Intelligence, Vice-Admiral Rufus L. Taylor, Jr. In 1966 Vice-Admiral Taylor was appointed Deputy Director of the Defense Intelligence Agency, then, from 1966 to 1969, served as Deputy Director of the Central Intelligence Agency. In the 1990s, when the Assassination Records Review Board (AARB) requested Taylor's files and records, it was reported that they were missing.

Lankford died in 1997 at age 75. His lengthy service as a Special Agent with the Office of Naval Intelligence is not mentioned in his obituaries published in the *Fort Worth Star-Telegram* and *Dallas Morning News*.

**Geneva and the HSCA**

On December 30 and 31, 1976, House Select Committee investigators Kevin Walsh and Jon Blackmer traveled from Washington D.C. to Paris, Texas to interview Roscoe White's widow, Geneva (now Mrs. Dees). After the two-day interview, Geneva allowed the investigators to take forty-two (42) items kept by her late husband.

Below right is a typed inventory of the items listed on the "Inventory of Roscoe White Photographs." The typed inventory lists this same item shown on the handwritten list.

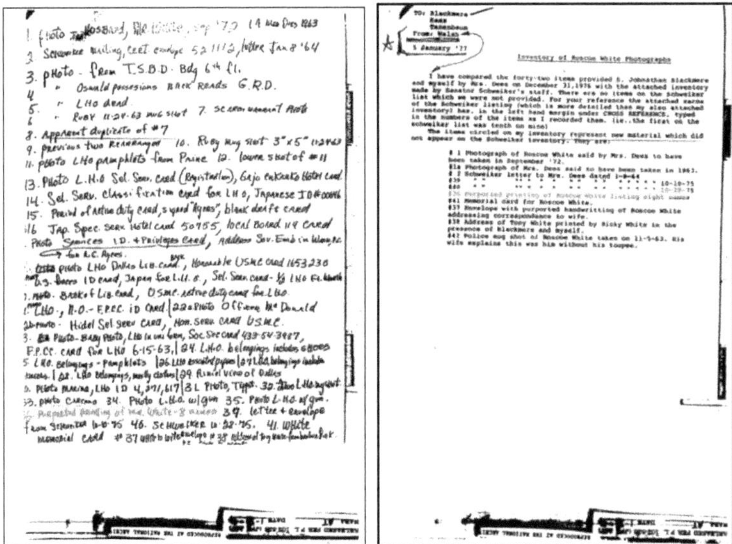

TO: Blackmere
Kass
Tanenbaum
From: Welsh
5 January '77

Inventory of Roscoe White Photographs

I have compared the forty-two items provided S. Johnathan Blackmere and myself by Mrs. Dees on December 31,1976 with the attached inventory made by Senator Schweiker's staff. There are no items on the Schweiker list which we were not provided. For your reference the attached xerox of the Schweiker listing (which is more detailed than my also attached inventory) has, in the left hand margin under CROSS REFERENCE, typed in the numbers of the items as I recorded them. (ie., the first on the Schweiker list was tenth on mine)

The items circled on my inventory represent new material which did not appear on the Schweiker inventory. They are:

# 1 Photograph of Roscoe White said by Mrs. Dees to have been taken in September '72.
#1a Photograph of Mrs. Dees said to have been taken in 1963.
# 2 Schweiker letter to Mrs. Dees dated 1-8-64
#39 " " " " " " " " " " " " 10-10-75
#40 " " " " " " " " " " " " 10-28-75
#36 Purported printing of Roscoe White listing eight names
#41 Memorial card for Roscoe White.
#37 Envelope with purported handwritting of Roscoe White addressing correspondance to wife.
#38 Address of Tony White printed by Ricky White in the presence of Blackmere and myself.
#42 Police mug shot of Roscoe White taken on 11-5-63. His wife explains this was him without his toupee.

*Geneva's handwritten list of materials surrendered to HSCA*

*Typed inventory of material provided to HSCA by Geneva.*

Item # 36, below left on the handwritten inventory, specifically identifies the item as *"Purported printing of Mr. White – 8 names."* The following photograph shows this handwritten list of names that Geneva provided to the HSCA. (Note: There are a total of **nine** (9) names listed on the page. For some reason the investigators failed to count the name "CPL SAMS" at the top of the list.) The authors are publishing this list in hopes someone may recognize these individuals and make known their connection, if any, with Roscoe White.

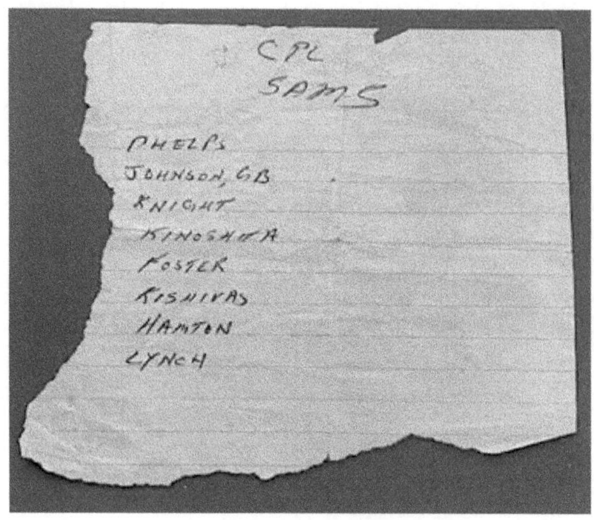

CPL
SAMS

PHELPS
JOHNSON, GB
KNIGHT
KINOSHITA
FOSTER
KISNIVAS
HAMTON
LYNCH

*Roscoe White's handwritten list of names.*

**More ONI on the Scene**

Two other Navy intelligence men appear to have played some role in the events in Dealey Plaza on the day of the assassination.

One was Captain David A. Sooy, who was "*... a lifelong officer in the USN and ONI and was Commander of the Dallas Naval Air Station for several years in the 1950s. When President John F. Kennedy was fatally shot in Dallas in November 1963, Captain Sooy was sitting in his car, waiting for the presidential motorcade to pass the school depository.*" (emphasis added) (Source: Find-A-Grave, Capt. David Aubrey Sooy).

Another was Lt. Gen. Richard E. Carey, *"...a Marine pilot stationed at the Dallas Naval Air Station was flying over downtown Dallas and the Dealey Plaza area at the time of the assassination.* (emphasis added) (Source: Sixth Floor Museum Oral History Collection, January 22, 1996.) *As a second lieutenant, he had been with General Douglas MacArthur on the way to Seoul in 1950. Carey would provide critical intelligence decisions enabling the successful defense of the Chinese attack on Hagaru-ri at the Chosin Reservoir."* (emphasis added). (Source: *The Flying Grunt* by Alan E. Mesches).

On Sunday, November 24, 1963, Cmdr. Robert D. Steel, USNR-R wrote a letter to Dallas Police Detective Paul Bentley stating that: *"...ONI (Office of Naval Intelligence) has quite a file on Oswald, which, no doubt has been made available on the Washington level. If not, I am certain that this information can be obtained for you through our resident special agent in charge of our Dallas office, A. C. Sullivan."*

Detective Bentley was one of the arresting officers who helped take Oswald into custody at the Texas Theatre. In his report, Bentley said that he was the one who removed Oswald's wallet which allowed them to learn his identity.

"A. C. Sullivan" is Arthur C. Sullivan mentioned above in connection to Lankford. Sullivan was well known to Dallas authorities having worked for the FBI and as an investigator for the Dallas District Attorney's office.

*Roscoe with three unidentified men.*

This photo of four men wearing swim trunks standing in the water was found among the personal effects of Roscoe White. Roscoe is second from the left. The man on Roscoe's right is believed to be an ONI agent who was stationed at Guantanamo Naval Base in Cuba in the early sixties. The identities of the other two men are not known.

*Beach at Guantanamo Bay, Cuba.*

The authors noted the "beach" photo of Roscoe, and the three unidentified men appears to have been taken from an elevated position. The photo above is of a beach at Guantanamo Naval Base with a wooden staircase in the background. Could the picture of the men have been taken by someone standing on this staircase? **IF** this photo was taken at Guantanamo, there is nothing in Roscoe's "official" military service records documenting that he was in Cuba at any time while in the Marines.

## AUTHENTICITY OF THE CABLES

There is no doubt in the minds of the authors that the age and provenance of the three messages lean heavily toward authenticity. Secondly, the "Navy Int." origin/sender designation was an obvious abbreviation for Naval Intelligence.

What about the message's validity? It bears consideration that a former Marine and CIA paramilitary intelligence officer, John Stockwell examined the cables and said that the formatting was *"not out of character"* and was similar to others he had seen while with the Agency. Stockwell had served with the CIA as Chief of Station and had received the CIA's Medal of Merit award.

In September 1990, Arthur D. Lujan came to the JFKAIC and spoke to J. Gary Shaw. Lujan said he was a Navy veteran who served in Vietnam and worked with the CIA. He said he had read about Ricky's father and asked if he could view the cables. After reading each cable, he told Shaw he had seen cables "*...like these many, many times...*" while serving with the Agency. He was particularly interested in the September cable that contained the sentence, *"Contacts are within in this letter."* He told Shaw, *"This could mean that a coded message was contained in the cable itself."*

So, while some have taken issue with the cable's format and language, including the misspelling of "Forgein" on cable #1 (Note: misspelling of words and names is common in official documents) it remains that Roscoe White may have been accustomed to receiving certain, perhaps off-the-grid, assignments in this format.

And, as he had done previously, he followed orders like a good soldier. He believed in his country and trusted in his superiors. He did his duty and carried out his assignments.

There was no reason for him to believe this assignment was any different from all his other successful operations.

And so, we are left in a quandary regarding the Roscoe White story. Are the cable messages real, or are they fake? Is this whole incident, as many have claimed, a complete hoax?

If they <u>are</u> real, then what next? The next chapter, The Mysterious "Scrapbook," may help in answering some of these intriguing questions.

*"Truth will ultimately prevail where there.*
*are pains taken to bring it to light."*

*— George Washington*

# CHAPTER SIX:
## The Mysterious "Scrapbook"

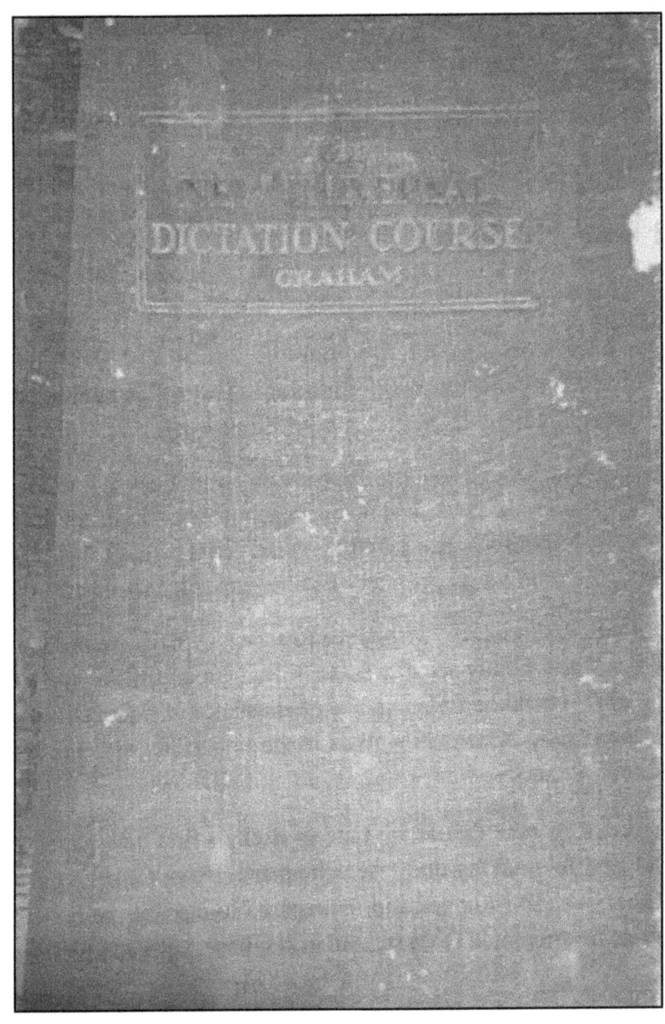


**FRONT COVER**

Among the items stored away in the tightly sealed metal canister was an old and falling apart small green shorthand textbook that Roscoe had converted into an almost childlike "scrapbook."

Therefore, since Roscoe died in 1971, it was at least nineteen years old when we first saw the book in 1990. It was much more readable when Ricky first showed it to us. The writing was more defined and legible. We could easily decipher the writings and scribblings and did our best to do so.

One of the questions that often arises when discussing the "scrapbook" is why we didn't allow others to examine it. The answer is simple; we were unsure as to what Roscoe's intentions were in creating and preserving the mysterious book. More importantly, the research tools now accessible to us, particularly the internet, were unavailable back then; and to be completely honest, we also wanted to keep it away from our government's criminal cover-up artists. After all, Roscoe's diary had already been illegally confiscated.

Furthermore, neither the co-authors nor Roscoe White's son Ricky understands a great deal of what is in this crudely crafted and puzzling "scrapbook." However, there is a lot we <u>do</u> know, <u>can</u> know — and <u>need</u> to know.

Firstly, one of our goals is to present the book just as it was found, along with our conclusions, observations, comments, and admittedly in some cases – conjecture.

Secondly, we request the reader's assistance in deciphering what Roscoe hoped to impart through his mysterious "scrapbook."

Undoubtedly, Roscoe worked secretly on the "scrapbook" and then hid it away. Before its discovery, no one had even seen the book, and no one remembers ever seeing Roscoe work with it. Obviously, its creator – Roscoe White – carefully preserved it and left it hidden for purposes known only to himself.

After careful thought, study, and research, we believe Roscoe may have created and hidden away the green book for personal and family security reasons. Later, regretful for his deed, perhaps he hoped that one day the book would be found and be of assistance in discovering, understanding, and perhaps exposing the real conspirators involved in the financially and politically motivated murder of President John F. Kennedy.

At this point, it is important to note that at the time of Ricky's first newspaper interview, very little time had been devoted to studying and researching the green book's contents. Therefore, Ricky, as he admitted later, was ill-equipped and unprepared to discuss the book's meaning and significance. Nevertheless, he attempted to do so, and in response, veteran investigative reporter Earl Golz wrote:

*"Less is known about what Ricky White says is a witness elimination list that he found in the cannister* [sic]. *Ricky White says there are 28 witnesses on the list, news clippings of each victim, and accompanied in some cases by his father's writing."* (*Austin American-Statesman*, 8/5/90, p. A12)

This statement was demonstrably untrue, and Ricky still regrets his uniformed, hasty reply to Golz's probing question. However, Ricky's misstatement – though disappointing and damaging to the scrapbook's credibility – does not negate the importance of the information found in the book. Furthermore, the authors firmly believe that the information gleaned from this book may eventually lead to heretofore unknown knowledge regarding both the motivation and participants involved in the assassination of President Kennedy.

**What We Do Know:**

The scrapbook was a 1920s-era dictation textbook with a faded, green-colored hardback cover. As previously noted, the book was already deteriorating and falling apart when Ricky pulled it out of the tightly sealed metal canister in 1990, at least 19 years after his father hid it.

The book's first 180 or so pages were missing. What happened to those missing pages is unknown. Of the remaining 62 pages, 25 had been utilized by Roscoe to paste in news clippings and scribble various pencil notations, numbers, and other markings. Ricky turned it over to us just as he found it. Of course, the question immediately arises – is it possible that at one time these missing pages contained information Roscoe did not feel comfortable leaving behind?

For some reason, in creating the "scrapbook," Roscoe turned the book upside down before adding the clippings and writings beginning at the <u>back</u> of the book. Accompanying the various pasted-in news-clipped photographs are scribbled pencil notations and code-like number sequences, many of which have thus far been indecipherable.

While its appearance indeed tends to diminish its credibility, the fact that it is so crudely done seems to bolster its authenticity — hence, its importance. Only 25 of the book's remaining 72 "upside-down" pages have been used for the pasted-in news clippings, scribbled pencil notations, numbers, and other markings. The remaining 47 pages were left blank.

The following pages have been presented here in the order they appear in the "scrapbook." The written description of the content of each page represents the authors' best effort to decipher this intriguing creation by the admitted assassin.

As noted, some of Roscoe's handwritten notations are relatively easy to read and understand, while others are illegible.

As will be readily seen, the front and back inside covers, and the cover's facing page contains some of the most important and informative notations found in the book.

**(NOTE: For convenience and reference, the pages of the book utilized by Roscoe have been numbered 2 through 25. The information contained on the inside of the front and back covers is considered as page 1.)**

**INSIDE FRONT COVER**

**INSIDE FRONT COVER:**

Looking at what is now the inside cover of the "upside-down book," the <u>FOCUS</u> of the "scrapbook" appears to be established with the handwritten words, ***"Players or witnesses."*** Also, written upside down at the top of this page is **"Page 121."** Page 121 is one of the missing pages.

What was Roscoe referring to? As will be seen, the answer is found in the first four pasted-in newspaper-clipped items.

At the bottom of this page, Roscoe wrote this number sequence:

**6 ' -- 28 6 ' 8 -- 69 -- 29 [illegible]**

**87 -- 62 -- 7 --97**

**1**

**PAGE 1:**

At the top of the inside front cover's facing page is the name of the scrapbook's OWNER (and creator), ***"R. A. White 1666106"*** – Roscoe's name and military identification number. A series of barely visible numbers (possibly an as-yet-unknown code?) are written at the bottom of the page.

**6 ' - 28 - 67  8 -  69 - 39 - 45**

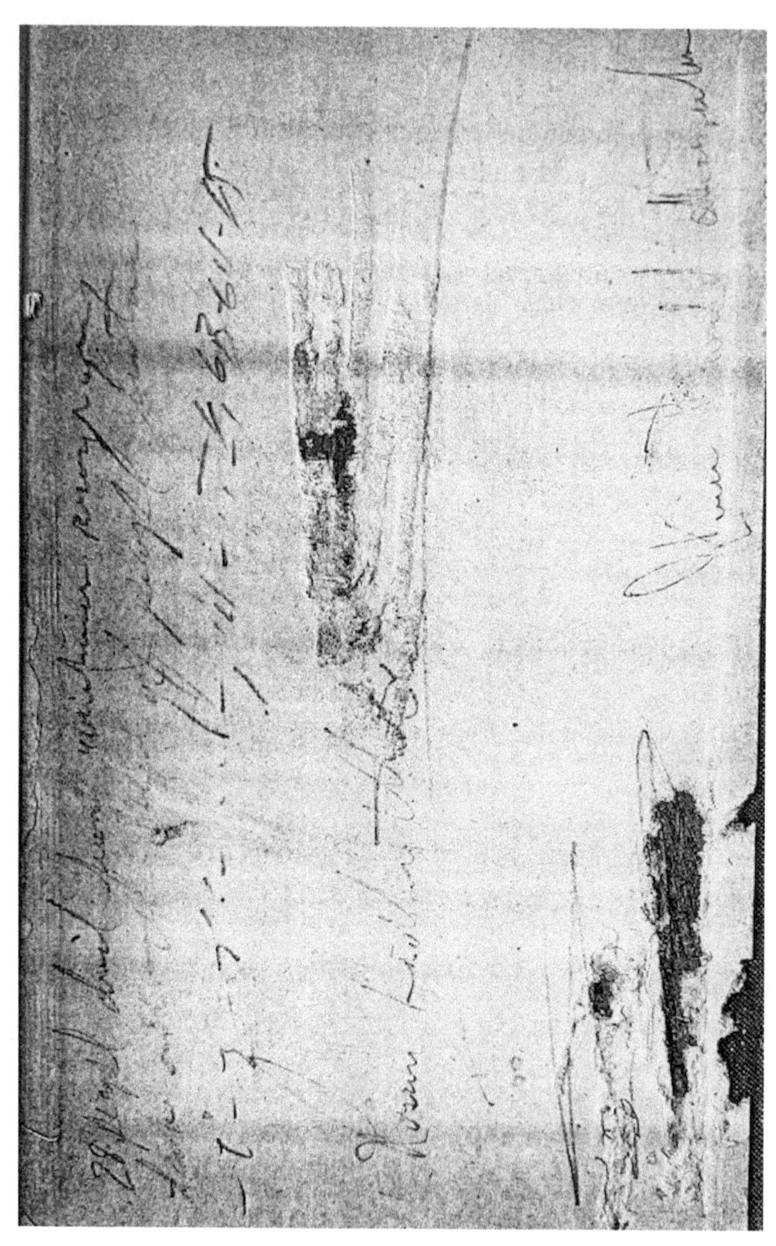

**INSIDE BACK COVER**

**INSIDE BACK COVER:**

Next, looking at what has now become the back inside cover, we find that the main TOPIC of the book is clearly and cryptically revealed. There, handwritten in pencil, Roscoe wrote this disturbing statement:

***"28 people died from witness program. Take out the rest of people later."***

Undoubtedly, this statement led to Ricky's misinterpretation of the scrapbook's contents.

Reading this statement and connecting it with the December plain text cable that ordered Roscoe to *"Stay within department, witnesses have eyes, ears and mouths….,"* we understand how Ricky initially believed this was "a witness elimination book." He first read about it in his father's stolen diary. It was also something that he discussed with Larry Ray Harris and Gary Shaw *before he found* the metal canister and the "scrapbook."

Underneath that grim and troubling statement lies the handwritten signature of the scrapbook's author, creator, and owner: ***"Roscoe Anthony White,"*** – who went by the codename of "MANDARIN," the recipient in the ominous "Navy Int." plain text cables discussed in the previous chapter. The third "Navy Int." message bearing a December 1963 date orders Roscoe to remain in the Dallas Police Department and monitor the assassination investigation and its witnesses.

Undoubtedly, Roscoe left behind this mysterious "scrapbook" fully intending that it be discovered, which leads one to consider:

> – What did Roscoe White want those who found the book to know and understand?
> – As an admitted participant in the assassination, what message was he trying to convey?

There has been no hesitation on the part of the authors to publish the contents of the scrapbook. It has been seen and studied only by a few researchers, and its contents have never been published or shown to the public. The authors hope that someone might interpret the random numbers and notations and help unravel any additional clues regarding the assassination, thereby facilitating a fuller understanding of the scrapbook's contents.

## The Subject Matter of the Scrapbook

The pasted-in content of the first four pages informs readers that the scrapbook's subject matter centers on people and events surrounding the assassination of President John F. Kennedy on November 22, 1963, in Dallas, Texas.

**THE FOLLOWING IS THE AUTHORS' PAGE-BY-PAGE REVIEW AND ASSESSMENT OF THE SCRAPBOOK.**

B—A • • • Monday, June 13, 1966—DALLAS TIMES HERALD

RUBY ARRIVES FOR HEARING

Jack Ruby, center, was quiet and subdued Monday as he arrived in the basement of the new county courthouse for his sanity hearing. Escorting him from the jail was Sheriff Bill Decker, left.—Staff Photo.

**PAGE 2:**

The first news-clipped photo comes from the June 13, 1966, edition of the *Dallas Times Herald.* It shows a pugnacious-looking Jack Ruby arriving at the courthouse for his court-ordered sanity hearing. This hearing was to appeal his conviction and death sentence for killing Oswald. In the foreground is Dallas County Sheriff Bill Decker. The date of the clipping gives us some idea of the time frame for the scrapbook's creation.

There are three long pencil strokes across the photo. As will be noted, these pencil strokes are a recurring pattern throughout the book, but their exact meaning is unclear.

A handwritten notation appears at the bottom of this page.

**good man die for good right…?**

Below the notation is another series of numbers.

**4" 8 - - 2 - 4 - 811 - 24**

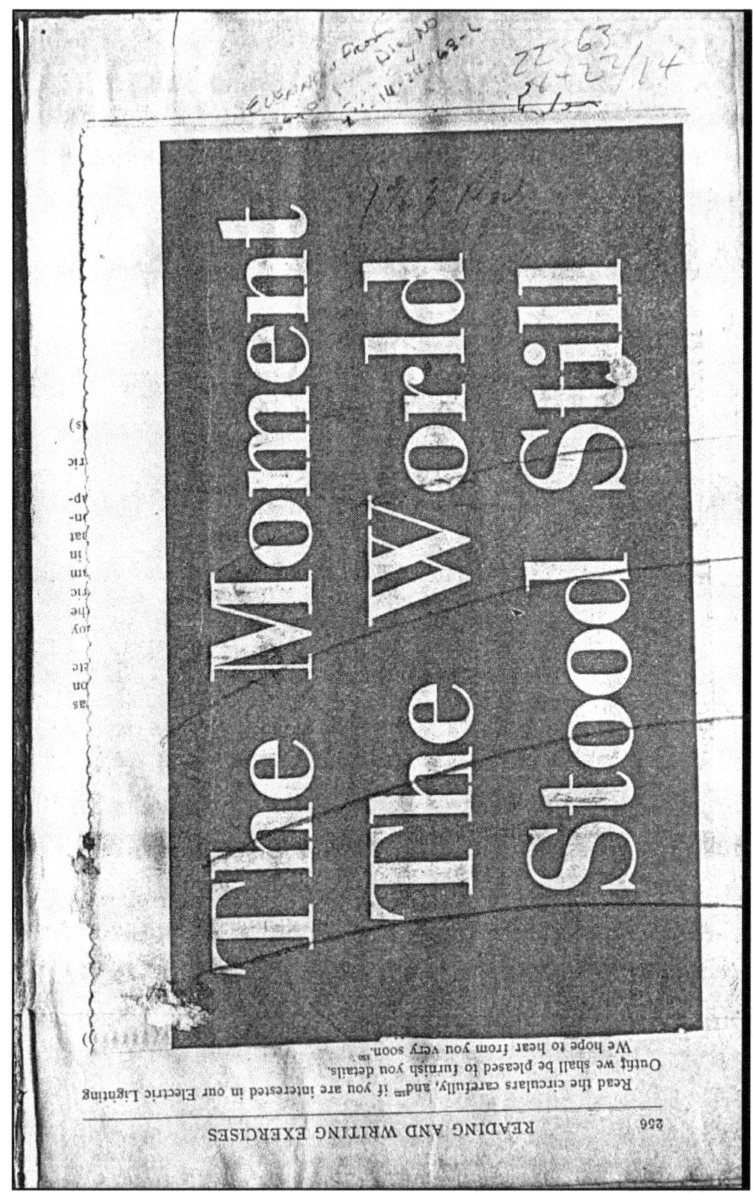
The Moment
The World
Stood Still
266 READING AND WRITING EXERCISES
Read the circulars carefully, and if you are interested in our Electric Lighting
Outfit we shall be pleased to furnish you details.
We hope to hear from you very soon.

**3**

**PAGE 3:**

This news-clipped headline is from an unknown source.

**The Moment The World Stood Still**

There are four long pencil strokes across the clipping, and a barely visible penciled-in date is present in the clipping's dark background.

**1963 NOV**

Above the headline news-clipping are hand-written notations appearing to read —

**Even now from**
**Bay of Pigs DI. NO**
**. . - - . "**
**-Feb. 14 - 24 - 63 - (**
**22 - 63**
**8 - 22 / 14**

Perhaps Roscoe is connecting this headline with the infamous and ill-fated CIA-planned Cuban Bay of Pigs invasion and attacking JFK's handling of the Cuban situation as the motive for his murder. The notations "**DI.**" and "**NO**" may be a reference to Dallas and New Orleans, key cities involved in some of the operational aspects of JFK's murder.

4

**PAGE 4:**

This news photo is of President Kennedy and his brother, U.S. Attorney General Robert Kennedy. The photo was taken during the McClellan Senate Hearings on Improper Activities of Labor sessions. There is one long pencil stroke across the heads of both men. Along the bottom margin, Roscoe wrote:

***Now got THE HeAD – going tail latter*** [sic]
**- 1 - 1/6 - 24 - 66**

(Note: This particular veiled threat, aimed at the two Kennedy brothers, is attributed to New Orleans Mafia boss Carlos Marcello. Reports of his making this statement were not in the public domain until sometime after 1971 and after Roscoe White's death. How did Roscoe know of this phrase?)

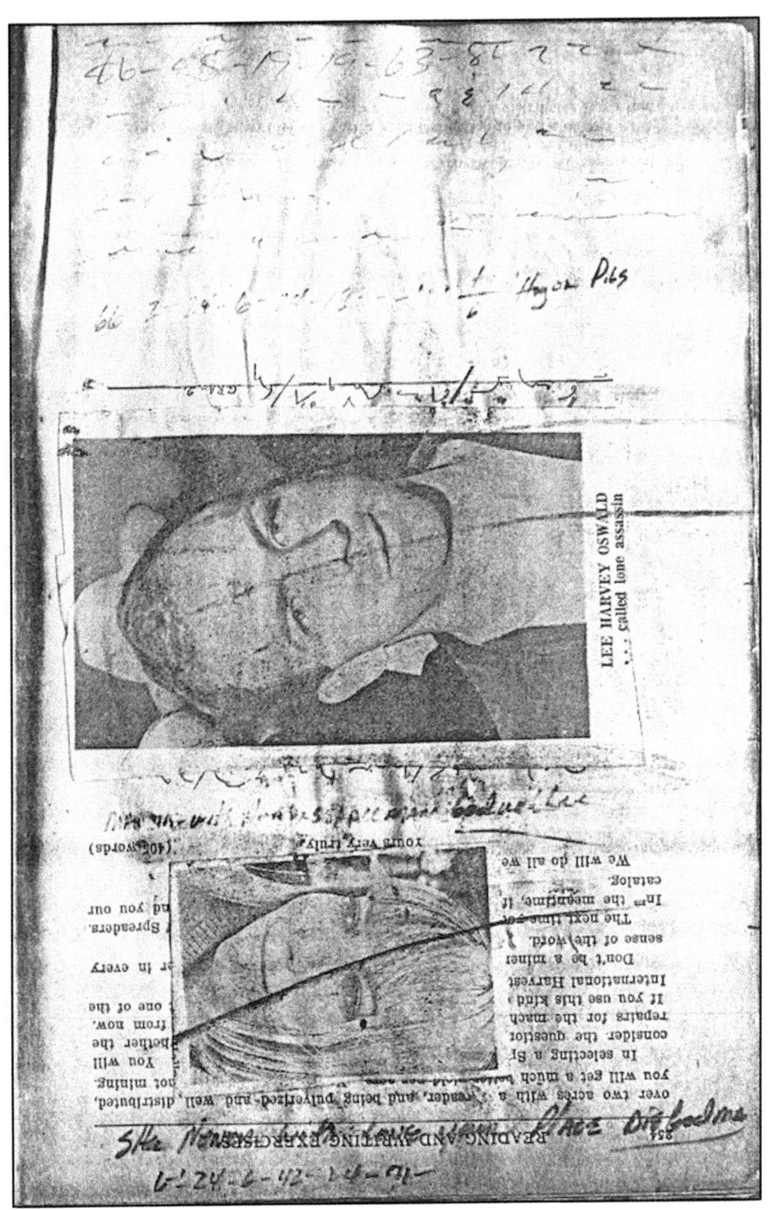


**5**

**PAGE 5:**

Several rows of partially legible handwritten number sequences and symbols are written at the top of this page.

^ - ^ - - ^ ^

**86 - 45 - 19- 19- 63 - 81** ^ ^ -

- - . - - - **a & 1 4** ^ . ^

**6 - 1** - [illegible]

[illegible]

**66 - ' 2 . . 24 - 6 - 24 - 18 - - - . . 1 / 6 'Hoy on P.65**

Below this is a news-clipped photo of accused assassin Lee Harvey Oswald with the caption: "Lee Harvey Oswald . . . called lone assassin." There is a long pencil stroke across his face.

Underneath Oswald's photo, Roscoe wrote –

**MAN DIE with Honor as ALL MAN GoduckLee** [sic]

A photo of an unidentified young, attractive blonde-headed woman is pasted on the page below Oswald's photo with one long pencil stroke across her face. A handwritten notation below this photograph reads —

**She** [three illegible words] **LOVE youR PlACE DiE God me** [sic]

*(left) photo from scrapbook;*
*(right) Mariella Novotny*

The woman is believed to be Mariella Novotny (real name: Stella Marie Capes). Author H. B. Albarelli writes the following in his revealing book, *Coup In Dallas*:

*"The FBI's record of the Profumo affair* [a major scandal in 20th-century British politics which involved Ms. Novotny] *is extensive and, not surprisingly, still heavily redacted* (at least as of 2019)*, and again it reveals failings on the part of JFK and others in his administration. That President Kennedy had dalliances with at least two of the women* [one being Ms. Novotny] *at the center of the Profumo affair is well documented by the investigative record."*

The record, Albarelli continues, also reveals that Novotny worked as a high-class prostitute in New York and London.

According to United States and European law enforcement authorities, she was considered a serious national security risk.

In November 1980, Novotny stated that she was writing her autobiography and that it would include details of a *"plot to discredit Jack Kennedy."* She also stated that she *"had kept a diary of all my appointments in the UN building. Believe me it's dynamite. It's now in the hands of the CIA."*

Unfortunately, the book never appeared. Novotny was found dead in February 1983, purportedly of a drug overdose. She was 42. Some thought she was murdered by American or British agents. Stephen Dorrel, a British politician, reported that: *"Shortly after her death, her house was burgled and her files and large day-to-day diaries from the early sixties to the seventies were stolen."*

More handwritten number series appear at the bottom of the page.

**6 ' - 24 - 6 - 42 -24 -71 -**

READING AND WRITING EXERCISES 253

No constitutional objection arises in this case, hence the court has the power to fund any indebtedness that the terms of the present act do not affirmatively or by fair implication prohibit. The words in this act being general, to-wit: "and judgment, the court in our opinion would not be justified in placing the limitation upon the kind of judgment that could be funded. That is, by construing the act to mean that only judgments rendered upon bonds are entitled to be funded. For such is not the meaning of the words used.

In fact, the words used are so comprehensive as not to require construction, and this is emphasized by the fact that the original act of '79 ... sively establishes the fact that the leg... was fully advised of how to place such limitations up... the legislatu...

It is ... the purpose ... there is no ... of the act, and ... ue of the provi... dness including ... ds are in the dis... more appropria... ties to fund not ... whether such judg... words, it seems t...

In th... to the fact that t... on that all the se... ns, and as to wha... , were absolutely ... provid-ing for

... words)

A sal... armer:

Mr. J. C. ...

D...

Dear Mr. ...

Are y... Well, there are ...

They ... farmer, not a min...

In mi... ll gone, and then ...

Now, ... nothing to give ba... ing his land—taking all of ... fertility away.

The land can be restored by careful nursing and fertilizing after it has been impoverished by this mining process, but the farmer would experience a great loss while it is being done.

Why allow the farm to get in this condition? It means a certain loss. A Manure Spreader will prevent this condition. There is always a disposition to put off this work of fertilizing, because it is a slow and tedious task.

With an International Harvester Spreader you can do in an hour what would require the better part of a day, and you avoid all of the disagreeable part of the work. It will do away with your inclination to put it off.

This Spreader thoroughly pulverizes the manure and distributes it, so that

**PAGE 6:**

This news-clipped photo is from the October 5, 1966, edition of the *Dallas Times Herald.* It shows three judges of the Texas Court of Criminal Appeals: W. A. Morrison, W. T. McDonald, and K. K. Woodley. In a unanimous opinion, this court had just overturned Jack Ruby's murder conviction and death sentence. They also ordered that Ruby be given a new trial at a location other than Dallas. However, Ruby died two months later — still in Dallas — having never received his new trial.

A handwritten statement appears at the top of this page.

**We soon have to go with sham** [sic] **you know**

This statement probably refers to the "sham" [fraud] of the "lone assassin, lone avenger" scenario.

Above and below the photo are several lines of thus-far illegible handwritten notations.

252 READING AND WRITING EXERCISES

before[875] them as incorporated in the revised statutes, with the act of 1879, they certainly would not have changed the language as it is to[900] be found in the present law, but would have re-adopted the language of the original act concerning the meaning of which there can be no[925] doubt. And by changing the language in the act of 1889 it must be presumed that the legislature intended to change the law.[950]

Again the language "including any judgments, bonds, or coupons" in the present act, of course, means the same as it meant in the original act[975] of 1889. In 1889 before the bonds could be issued, except in those counties in which the bonds had been funded, and a[1000] vote of the people had, no bond could be issued without a

**7**

**PAGE 7:**

This news-clipped photo is of Jack Ruby seated and surrounded by several men. The man on the far left is Dallas County Sheriff Bill Decker. The man wearing eyeglasses standing next to Decker is John McKee, President of the Greater Dallas Crime Commission at the time of Ruby's trial. His real name was James Kell Zullinger.

*James Kell Zullinger, aka John McKee*

There is a single pencil check mark next to McKee's left ear; the stroke continues across the face of the unidentified man standing to his left.

The McKee/Zullinger story is an intriguing one and worthy of mention here.

James Kell Zullinger deserted the U.S. Navy in 1929. A year later, after changing his name to John McKee, he moved to Dallas. In 1935 he began work for the Ford Motor Company and retired in 1971. His title with Ford was Regional Manager, Civic Affairs. He later became the second-ranking officer in the Texas Masonic organization and President of the Scottish Rite Hospital for Crippled Children in Dallas, Texas.

As head of the Dallas Crime Commission, McKee was interviewed by the FBI the day after Ruby shot Oswald. He furnished them with a listing of Ruby's violations and citations since 1954. McKee was previously interviewed by the FBI in 1962 and was reported by them to be: " *...a very good friend of this bureau and was unusually cooperative"* (emphasis added). McKee was quoted as saying that *"... he believes Jack Ruby can receive a fair trial in Dallas."*

In early January 1969, McKee told authorities that informers warned him that James Walter Cherry had taken a contract to kill him. This statement came shortly after Cherry was arrested for murdering Dallas Sheriff Deputy Buddy Walthers on January 10, 1969. Walthers was a very active and controversial law enforcement officer associated with events surrounding the assassination of President Kennedy and the shooting of Oswald.

McKee's attorney was William F. Alexander, a name well-known to Kennedy researchers. At the time of the assassination, he was Dallas District Attorney Henry Wade's Chief assistant. (Note: FBI informant and lone-nut advocate Hugh Aynesworth wrote a lengthy, revelatory article about the McKee/Zullinger affair in the August 1983 issue of *D Magazine.*)

Two lines of hand-scribbled notations are above the photo.

**84 - 16 - 26 - ^ ^ ^ 16**

**28 12. ' - - ^ - 18 ^ ^**

READING AND WRITING EXERCISES 251

redeem, and cancel bonds as the same are called for redemption," might fairly be said to support the theory that only judgment on bonds were entitled to be included. But notwithstanding the above facts a review of the history of this legislation impels me to the opinion that any judgment whether rendered on bonds or not, can be funded under this act. The original act was passed in 1879, sessions act of 1879, page 1, chapter ... 1879 vol. 2, page 848. The language used in the original ... be funded, after specifically me...

8

**PAGE 8:**

The man in this photo has yet to be identified. He has a thick crop of either blonde or gray hair, maybe wearing a toupee, and is wearing dark horn-rimmed glasses. There are two pencil strokes across his face. The man bears some resemblance to this 1930 picture of New Orleans Attorney Maurice Brooks Gatlin. **IF** the photo **IS** of Gatlin, he is connected to some of the mysterious events associated with the murder of President Kennedy. Here is a summary of what is known about him.

Gatlin is reported to have gone to France in 1962 to pass $100,000 in CIA funds to assist an unidentified French rightist organization's attempt to assassinate President De Gaulle (Turner, William; *The Garrison Commission,* pp.47 and 61). This rightist organization likely included a French assassin named Jean Rene Souetre, who was in Dallas on the day of President Kennedy's assassination. Souetre was expelled from the United States within 48 hours after the assassination. These expulsion orders came from Washington.

*Maurice Brooks Gatlin*

On May 28, 1965, two and a half years after the assassination, Gatlin either jumped, fell, or was pushed from a 6th-floor balcony of the Caribe Hilton Hotel in San Juan, Puerto Rico. Just a little over six months after the assassination, Guy Banister, Gatlin's close associate, was found dead on June 6, 1964. (Note: Oswald had worked out of Bannister's office while in New Orleans.)

*The San Juan Caribe Hotel in 1965.*

The photo below shows some of the heavily redacted Maurice Gatlin FBI files received by J. Gary Shaw from the agency in the early 1980s in response to his Freedom of Information request. (Note: During the House Select Committee's investigation, Gatlin's New Orleans FBI files were destroyed by the agency in November and December 1977.)

*FBI's file on Maurice Gatlin.*

The second photo on this scrapbook page is of a dark-haired woman bearing a strong resemblance to another of President Kennedy's so-called "girlfriends," Ellen "Ella" Rometsch (real name, Bertha Hildegard Ella). She was thought to be a Soviet spy and a national security risk.

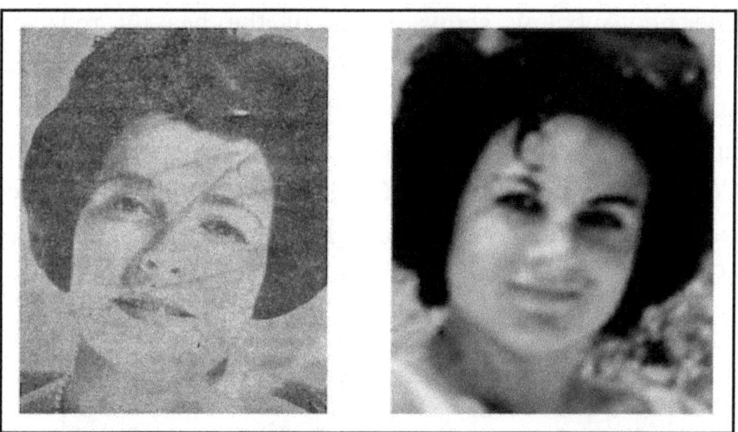

*(left) Photo from scrapbook, and (right)*
*Ellen Rometsch*

In the photo from the scrapbook, there are four pencil strokes across her face, and below her photo is another number sequence.

**24 - 66 - 4 - 28**

Above and along the side of the two photos are mostly illegible numbers and pencil scribblings.

It is interesting to note that in May 1963, six months before the assassination, Mrs. Rometsch accompanied Bobby Baker, Vice-President Johnson's right-hand man, to New Orleans. Also on the trip were Baker's secretary, Nancy Carole Tyler, and Puerto Rico mortgage banker Paul Aguirre. After New Orleans, the group continued to Miami and Dallas. (Note: During this same time, Lee Harvey Oswald moved to New Orleans.)

When questioned by investigators for the Washington-based Senate Rules Committee that investigated Bobby Baker's affairs, banker Paul Aguirre stated that if he *". . . were asked anything about what took place* [on the trip to New Orleans] *he would take all the amendments from 1 to 28."* (Source: Albarelli, H. B. Jr., *Coup in Dallas,* p. 133). Later, in July 1963, the FBI questioned Rometsch and concluded that she probably was a Soviet spy. The next month she and her husband, a military attaché at the West German Embassy, were deported to Germany.

Additionally, it has been alleged that then-Congressman Gerald Ford utilized the services of Rometsch while he served on the Warren Commission investigating the JFK assassination.

In May 1965, Carole Tyler, Ms. Rometsch's travel companion, died in a plane crash in Maryland. She was 26. Four years later, in July 1969, Tyler's roommate Mary Jo Kopechne died at Chappaquiddick Island, Massachusetts. She "drowned" in an automobile "accident" while riding with JFK's brother Senator Edward Kennedy. She was only 28 years old.

For the record, Mafia boss Carlos Marcello's childhood friend and business associate, Nick Popich, hosted Baker and his entourage at his restaurant while they were in New Orleans. Additionally, and suspiciously, in August 1963, a man matching Popich's description was seen by a reliable witness in Dallas at the Carousel Club with Jack Ruby and Lee Oswald.

They were seen meeting together with Texas Governor John Connally, another man called Chuck, and a Dallas detective – who happened to be walking just behind Oswald when he was shot by Ruby. The witness stated that at the same meeting, he observed an open suitcase full of money on Ruby's desk.

As of this writing, Mrs. Rometsch is still alive and well. For more information on her connection to the JFK case refer to the eye-opening book, *COUP IN DALLAS, The Decisive Investigation into Who Killed JFK* by H. P. Albarelli, Jr. with Leslie Sharp and Alan Kent (2021). In one of the book's back-cover reviews, J. Gary Shaw wrote:

*"An impressive and staggering piece of investigative journalism. Based upon the jotted-down notations found in the 1963 datebook of an amoral clandestine government henchman* [Pierre Lafitte, see photos below]*, we now know the identities of some of the planners and perpetrators of the Crime of the Century."*

*Photo array of Pierre Lafitte*

*Coup in Dallas* is based primarily on Lafitte's 1963 datebook. Therein, Ellen Rometsch's name appears thirteen times between the dates of June 16 and October 18.

**PAGE 9:**

At the top of the page are these notations:

[Illegible] **1968** [Illegible]
[Illegible] **1 2** [Illegible]

Below these notations are two news-clipped photos. The top photo is of an unidentified masculine-looking blonde or gray-headed woman. This person bears a strong resemblance to female impersonator Harvey W. Goodwin. When on stage, Goodwin was always introduced as *"The Incredible MR. HARVEY LEE."* (Note: Goodwin often performed at *Club My O My,* a popular New Orleans tourist attraction.)

There are four pencil strokes across the face. The reason for Goodwin's presence in the green book is unknown; he is *NOT* one of the *"28 people* [who] *died from witness program."* Goodwin was 79 years old when he died in 1992 – 21 years after Roscoe was killed.

The authors can only speculate as to why this photo is included in Roscoe White's perplexing scrapbook. Could Roscoe be alluding to his knowledge that there were two Oswalds involved in the assassination?

John Armstrong, in his extraordinarily researched book, *Harvey and Lee*, makes an exceptionally strong case for there having been two Oswalds who played active roles in the events of November 22, 1963. One used the name **Lee Harvey** Oswald, while the other was known as **Harvey Lee** Oswald.

*(clockwise from top left) masculine-looking woman from scrapbook – female impersonator, "The Fabulous Mr. Harvey Lee," – Harvey Lee Goodwin – 1960's era, Club My O My program.*

Therefore, could this inclusion of female impersonator Mr. Harvey Lee be an admission of Roscoe's association with both men? If so, it appears that Roscoe intended to expose the "Two Oswalds" charade that was part of the assassination operation. Armstrong believes that it was HARVEY LEE Oswald, not Lee Harvey Oswald, who was employed at the Texas School Book Depository at the time of the assassination.

Not surprisingly, the Assassination Records Review Board discovered that at one time there existed an FBI file numbered 105-2137 captioned "**Harvey Lee** Oswald." That file is now MISSING!

The bottom photo on this page shows two as yet unidentified men in suits sitting at what appears to be a desk or table. They may be Warren Commission staff members who came to Dallas tasked with deposing various witnesses. Each man has a pencil stroke across his face. A hand-scribbled notation is below the photo.

**Cover-up starts now**

This is an obvious reference by Roscoe inferring that the Warren Commission's responsibility was to ensure the "lone assassin," "lone avenger" scenario remained intact.

READING AND WRITING EXERCISES 249

American citizens act within their indisputable rights in taking their ships and in traveling wherever their legitimate business calls them upon the high seas, and exercise those rights in what should be the well-justified confidence that their lives will not be endangered by acts done in clear violation of universally acknowledged international ...

... disavow the acts of which the Government of the United States complains; that they will make reparation so far as reparation is possible for injuries which are without measure, and that they will take immediate steps to prevent the recurrence of anything so obviously subversive of the principles of warfare for which the Imperial German Government have in the past so wisely and so firmly contended.

JOHN F. KENNEDY
. . . reluctant peacemaker

LYNDON JOHNSON
. . . disagreement reported

**PAGE 10:**

At the top of this page, Roscoe wrote,

[Illegible]
[Illegible] **Peace with world**
**learn wisdom**

These notations are followed by four news-clipped photos:

- President Kennedy captioned: JOHN F. KENNEDY . . . reluctant peacemaker.
- Vice-President Johnson captioned: LYNDON JOHNSON . . . disagreement reported.
- Below these are caption-less photos of Texas Senator Ralph Yarbrough and Texas Governor John Connally.

To the left of JFK's photo is an illegible handwritten notation, and additional notations at the bottom of the page.

The photo of JFK is unmarked, while LBJ's photo has a large check mark on his face. The photos of Yarborough and Connally have large pencil marks across their faces. This clipping may suggest one of the primary reasons for the President's trip to Texas; specifically, the trip was an attempt to heal a deep division in the Texas Democratic Party. Two deeply divided Democratic factions existed at the time: (1) the conservative wing led by Texas Governor Connally, and (2) the liberal wing led by Senator Ralph Yarborough. These men were the four leading political figures in Texas who rode in the Dallas motorcade.

248 READING AND WRITING EXERCISES

sumes, on the[37] contrary, that the Imperial German Government accept, as of course, the rule that the lives of non-combatants, whether they be of neutral citizenship or citizens of[38] one of the nations at war, cannot lawfully or rightfully be put in jeopardy by the … or destruction of … unarmed merchantman, and recognize[39] also, as all … the usual precaution of visit and search, … is in[40] fact of belligerent nationalit… under a neutral flag.

The Governmen… call the attention of the Imperial Germ… the fact that the objection to their pres… lies in …e practical impossibil… of commerce …ithout disregarding … which all modern opinion … for the officers of a submarine … papers and cargo. It is practical… and, if they cannot put a[41] … leaving her crew and all o… boats. These facts it is unde…

We are informed that in … instance… have spoken, time e… for even that poor measure of safety was … in at least two of the cases cited not[42] so much as a warning was … Manifestly, submarines not be used against merchantmen, as the last … weeks have shown, without an inevitable violation[43] of many sacred principles of justice and humanity.

**PAGE 11:**

The news-clipped photo on this page is of President Abraham Lincoln. His head appears to have been torn off.

Above the photo of Lincoln is the number **1** with a circle around it, and at the bottom of the page is the number **26** followed by a short dash:

Interestingly, a Lincoln-head penny with a hole through the head of President Lincoln's image was found taped inside the previously mentioned 1963 datebook of Pierre Lafitte.

As recounted in Albarelli's *Coup in Dallas*, the datebook contains information about the people and activities directly related to the Kennedy assassination. Was this news clipping a grizzly comparison between the Lincoln and Kennedy assassinations, possibly suggesting that the motives for both murders were somehow related?

*Penny taped inside Pierre Lafitte's datebook.*

Also, of interest within the above-mentioned, government henchman Pierre Lafitte's datebook are two entries referencing someone named "White." Below is the first entry dated January 24, 1963.

**848 - HARVEY - SOON**
**WHITE - SMITH**
**(CANADA)**

Recall that in February 1963, Roscoe received the first of his three "Navy Int." messages containing orders that his foreign affairs assignments had been canceled and that his next assignment would occur in one of three Texas cities — Houston, Austin, or Dallas. His new assignment was to "…. *eliminate a National Security threat to world wide peace."* The second Lafitte *Datebook* entry involving someone named White is dated December 9, 1963.

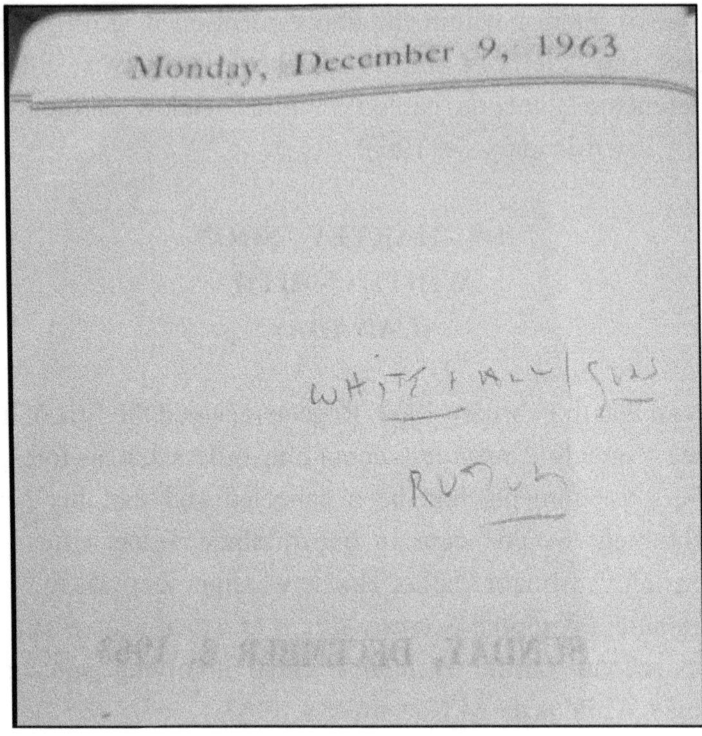


*Entry in Lafitte's datebook for December 9, 1963*

**White + all / guns Rudel**

The third "Navy Int." message, dated December 1963, ordered Roscoe to remain in the Dallas Police Department and monitor the assassination investigation and associated witnesses. Are these "White" references in Lafitte's datebook about Roscoe White? **If** – as *Admitted Assassin* contends – Roscoe White's admission of guilt in the assassination of JFK is true, then it stands to reason that his name would appear along with other players found in a datebook that reveals the participants and actions of those involved in this ruthless and brutal operation.

READING AND WRITING EXERCISES 247

Imperial German Government to its naval commanders to be upon the same plane of humane action prescribed by the naval codes of other nations, the Government of the United States was loath to believe—it cannot now bring itself to believe—that these acts, so absolutely contrary to the rules, practices, and the spirit of modern warfare, could have the countenance or sanction of that great Government. It feels it to be its duty, therefore, to address the Imperial German Government concerning them with the utm[...] fran[...] and in the earnest hope that it is not mistaken in expecting action o[...] Imperial German Government, which will correct the unfortunat[...] have been created, and vindicate once more the position of th[...] to the sacred freedom of the seas.

[...] cut Germany off from all [...] adopt methods of retaliation which go [...]uch beyond the ordinary m[...] warfare at sea, in the proclamation of a war [...]ne from which they have [...] neutral ships to keep away. This Government [...]s already taken occasion to [...] the Imperial German Government that it can[...]t admit the adoption of s[...] ures or such warning of danger to operate as any degree an abbreviation [...] rights of American shipmasters or of Amer[...] citizens bound on lawful [...] as passengers on merchant ships of bellig[...]t nationality, and that it must [...] the Imperial German Government to a strict accountability for any infringement of those rights, intentional or incidental. It does understand the Imperial German Government to question those rights. It as-

**PAGE 12:**

There are two lines of scribbling and markings at the top of this page.

**26 - 84 - 76 ‘ 2** [illegible]
[illegible]

Below the scribblings is a news-clipped photo of Texas Governor John B. Connally shaking the hand of an unidentified man while an unidentified Hispanic-looking man looks on.

As of now, the reasoning behind Roscoe including this photo in his “scrapbook” is unclear. There are no visible pencil marks on this photo.

246 READING AND WRITING EXERCISES

President Wilson's Note to Germany

the side of justice and humanity; and having understood the instructions of the

**PAGE 13:**

Roscoe made the following notation at the top of this page,

**murder you** [illegible]
[illegible]

Below these scribblings is a news-clipped photo of former Vice-President Lyndon Johnson being sworn in on *Air Force One* as the new president by Federal Judge Sarah Hughes. Mrs. John F. Kennedy is on Johnson's left, while Dallas Police Chief Jesse Curry – mostly hidden from view by LBJ's raised right hand – is in the background on his right. White House Aide Kenneth O'Donnell and others look on from behind Mrs. Kennedy. There are several pencil strokes around the heads of LBJ and O'Donnell.

READING AND WRITING EXERCISES 245

KEY TO THE PLATE ON THE OPPOSITE PAGE

The use of long words which we get from other tongues not only makes our thoughts and our speech dim and hazy, but it has done somewhat to harm the morals of our people. Crime sometimes does not look like crime when it is set before us in the many folds of a long word. When a man steals and we call it "defalcation," we are at a loss to know if it is a blunder or a crime. If he does not tell the truth and we are told that it is a case of "prevarication," it takes us some time to know just what we should think of it.

No man will ever cheat himself into wrong-doing, nor will he be at a loss to judge of ... ers if he thinks and speaks of acts in clear, crisp, English term... is a good rule, ...en one is at a loss to know if an act is ri... or wrong, to wr... out in short straight-out Engl...

...

...tar, ... and learn ... thing in all parts of the house. There ... som...ing of the ... gained when we try to use only short words; when we look them up we see a great many others, and learn a great many things about other topics as well. (1882 words)

**PAGE 14:**

At the top of this page are five lines of mostly illegible pencil notations and markings.

**28 - 16 - 16 - 20 -** [Illegible]
[Illegible]
[Illegible]
[Illegible]
[Illegible]

Below the notations is a June 8, 1967, news-clipped photo of President Johnson and West German Foreign Minister Willy Brandt before their meeting at the White House. According to UPI, *"Brandt, who has been conferring with U. S. officials, is the first member of the new West German Coalition Government under chancellor Kurt Kissinger to come to Washington."*

In August 1961, while Vice-President, Johnson met with Brandt in Bonn, Germany. UPI reported that the meeting ". . . *was to assure the people of free Germany of continued U.S. support in the Berlin crisis."*

Both men have penciled checkmarks on their heads.

This meeting probably pertained to JFK's position on the Berlin crisis and the USSR/USA conflict. President Kennedy's position on this crisis conflicted dramatically with his hawkish military advisers.

**15**

**PAGE 15:**

This is a news-clipped photo of Jack Ruby as he rushed forward to shoot and kill the handcuffed and defenseless accused assassin Lee Harvey Oswald while dozens of armed Dallas law enforcement officers stood idly by.

Underneath the photo, Roscoe wrote:

**16 - 24**
**7 ' ' ' 82 - 4**
**Set up job**
**Ruby was brave**

Oswald's head has been encircled in pencil, while Ruby's head has a penciled checkmark. Apparently, with these statements, *"Set up job"* and "*Ruby was brave,"* Roscoe was saying that Oswald's poorly protected transfer to the county jail and his execution was pre-planned and carried out by a "brave" Jack Ruby.

READING AND WRITING EXERCISES 243

version the word "brood" is used. Read the verse again with this term and you will feel its full force.

When Daniel Webster made a speech he used to tell those who put it in form for the press to strike out every long word. If you will study the things he said or wrote, you will find that they were mainly made up of short, clear, strong terms, although he sometimes used those ... No other man could paint ...

in English, but in Indian I say he is like an old tree, dead at the top, that tells it at once. That is the way we talk with one another in Indian, and we like it best."

So this little band stands out against our speech because their own is the most clear and simple to them. This shows how strong is the love of clear thoughts and clear ideas with all kinds of men. Those who wish to teach or lead others must first learn to think in a clear way.

**16**

**PAGE 16:**

There are a couple of illegible hand-scribbled notations at the top of this page.

The news-clipped photo is of accused assassin Lee Harvey Oswald while in custody at the Dallas Police Department. Detectives Elmer Boyd and M. G. Hall are in the background.

At the bottom of the page are two lines of notations; the first line is unreadable but on the second line, Roscoe wrote the name,

**amos Euins**

Amos Euins was an eyewitness to the assassination. He was 15 years old at the time, and with permission, left school to see the President. Amos was standing directly across Elm Street and facing the TSBD when the shots were fired. After the shooting, Amos gave somewhat differing accounts to officials about what he witnessed that day. One of his more problematic statements to the Warren Commission was that <u>he was not sure whether the man he saw in the window was white or black</u>. Euins was approached by a writer from *National Guardian* magazine (March 21, 1964). Amos refused to speak to the journalist because a Secret Service man warned that he would get in real trouble if he talked to anyone.

them. Take that which says, "Oh, ye generation of vipers, who hath
warned you" to flee from the wrath to come?" there is one long word
which ought not to be in it, namely, "generation." In the elder
ADDRESS ON THE USE OF SHORT WORDS—Continued
242 READING AND WRITING EXERCISES

**17**

**PAGE 17:**
This is a famous news-clipped photo of Dallas detective John C. Day holding a rifle above his head, displaying it for reporters and photographers. Reportedly, the rifle was found on the 6th floor of the Texas School Book Depository building.

Below this photo, Roscoe wrote,

**7.65 mauser**
**our gun**
**use kill**
**President Kennedy**
**Nov 22**
**1963**

With the phrase *"our gun use,"* Roscoe declares that the rifle being held by Day was NOT the gun used to kill JFK; rather, the actual weapon belonged to the owner and creator of this "scrapbook" – Roscoe Anthony White.

This is one of four instances wherein Roscoe admitted that he was one of JFK's killers – hence, this book's title, *Admitted Assassin.*

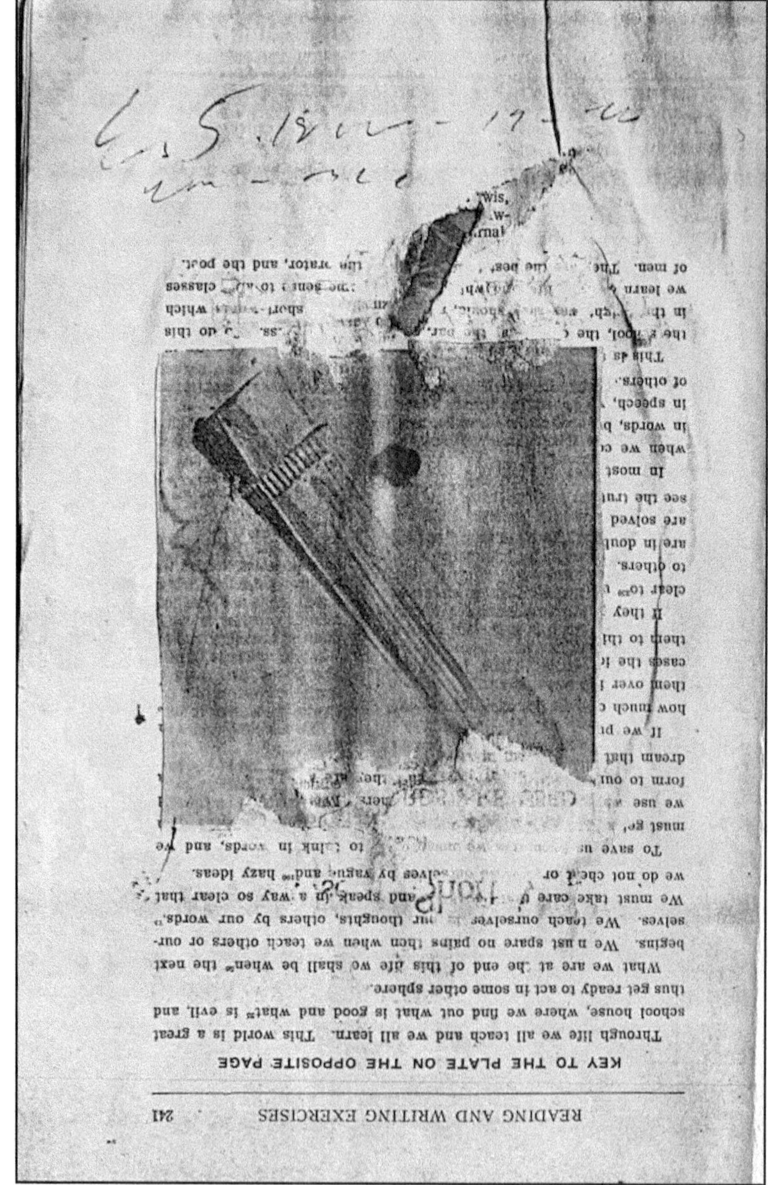

READING AND WRITING EXERCISES 241

**KEY TO THE PLATE ON THE OPPOSITE PAGE**

Through life we all teach and we all learn. This world is a great school house, where we find out what is good and what[35] is evil, and thus get ready to act in some other sphere.

What we are at the end of this life we shall be when[36] the next begins. We must spare no pains then when we teach others or ourselves. We teach ourselves [illegible] our thoughts, others by our words.[37] We must take care [illegible] and speak in a way so clear that we do not che[illegible] or [illegible]selves by vague and[38] hazy ideas.

To save u[illegible] to think in words, and we must ge[illegible] we use [illegible] form to ou[illegible] dream tha[illegible]

If we p[illegible] how much [illegible] them over [illegible] cases the [illegible] them to th[illegible]

If they [illegible] clear to[39] [illegible] to others. [illegible] are in dou[illegible] are solved [illegible] see the tru[illegible]

In most [illegible] when we c[illegible] in words, [illegible] in speech, [illegible] of others.

This is [illegible] the school, the [illegible] the bar, [illegible]ss. [illegible] do this in th[illegible] short-[illegible] which we learn [illegible] some sense to all classes of men. The [illegible] the best [illegible] the orator, and the poet.

**PAGE 18:**

This is a news-clipped photo of the 6.5 mm bullet that authorities alleged was responsible for seven wounds found on the president and governor. This photo may have been Roscoe's attempt to call attention to the

Roscoe wrote the following notation about this photo.

**6.5 mm - 17 - u**

[Illegible]

240 READING AND WRITING EXERCISES

AN ADDRESS

On the U[illegible] of [illegible] Words

IN [illegible]

ONL[illegible] SHORT [illegible]

**PAGE 19:**

This is a news-clipped photo of the seven Warren Commission members, and their chief counsel, J. Lee Rankin. This astute gang, along with governmental investigators, was responsible for concocting the absurd and mythical “lone-assassin” – “magic bullet” – and “lone-avenger” scenarios.

Below the photo, Roscoe wrote,

**protecting us**

With the statement *“protecting us,”* Roscoe appears to acknowledge that the prearranged responsibility of this carefully hand-picked presidential assassination commission was to omit, ignore, or revise all evidence pointing to multiple shooters and conspiracy.

There was nothing to worry about; the criminal cover-up was already in play.

THE LETTER BELOW IS THE KEY TO THE FOLLOWING PLATE
READING AND WRITING EXERCISES 239

**20**

**PAGE 20:**

Roscoe wrote the following words at the top of this page.

**Mandarin**
**kills K uses 7.65**
**mauser in assassination**

With these words, Roscoe ("Mandarin") once again admitted his role as an assassin of President Kennedy.

This news clip is a cropped version of the full Polaroid picture shown below. It was taken by bystander and eyewitness Mary Ann Moorman at the exact moment of the headshot. There are three pencil strokes across JFK and the limousine. At the upper left corner of the photo, atop the infamous picket fence, Roscoe located his firing position with a dot with an "X" marked through it.

Ken O'Donnell, former Special Assistant to President Kennedy, who rode in the Secret Service follow-up car directly behind the president, said:

*"I told the FBI that I heard [two shots from behind the grassy knoll fence], but they said it couldn't have happened that way and that I must have been imagining things. So I testified the way they wanted me to. I just didn't want to stir up any more pain and trouble for the family."*

O'Donnell died in 1977 just as the House Select Committee was investigating President Kennedy's assassination. He was 53 years old. (O'Neill, Thomas P. Jr.; *Man of the House*, p. 178)

Pencil scribblings, mostly illegible, are at the very bottom of the page. It's important to note that as on page 17, this statement appears to be another handwritten admission by Roscoe White, "Mandarin," that he shot the president.

Minutes after the assassination, police, and citizens ran to the area behind the picket fence and went directly to the exact location from which Roscoe admitted firing at the president. Both the policeman and the citizens discovered numerous footprints and cigarette butts in that area. (Note: Ricky said his father was a heavy smoker.)

***Top photo** – uncropped Moorman photo; **middle photo** – taken immediately after the assassination, toward Roscoe's claimed firing position at the picket fence; **bottom photo** – close-up of the middle photo showing police searching behind the picket fence.*

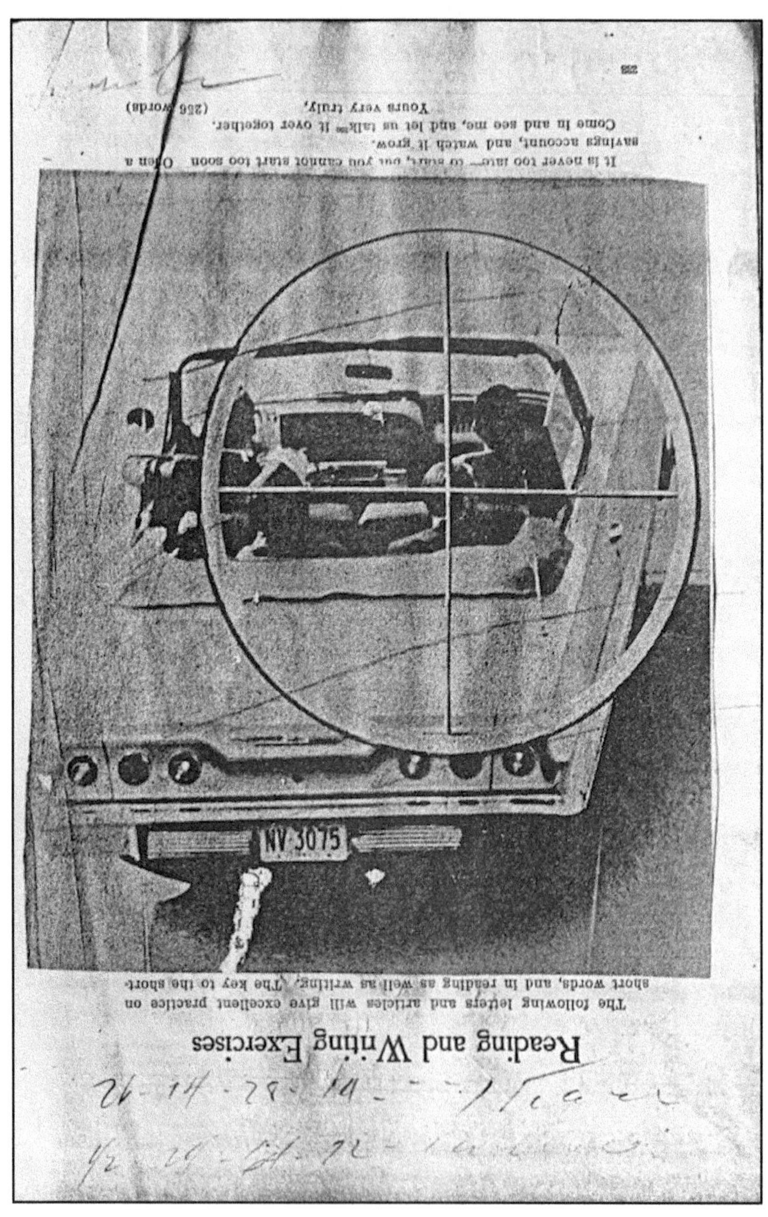

Reading and Writing Exercises

The following letters and articles will give excellent practice on short words, and in reading as well as writing. The key to the short-



It is never too late to start, but you cannot start too soon. Open a savings account, and watch it grow.

Come in and see me, and let us talk it over together.

Yours very truly, (256 words)

**PAGE 21:**

Roscoe wrote this word in the page's top margin.

**Lambs**

Considering the lack of protection given to the president that day in Dallas, "Lambs" – as in "lambs led to the slaughter" – stands alone as a succinct, single-word truth.

The news-clipped photo was taken November 27, 1963, during the Secret Service's reenactment (without gunfire) of the assassination. It shows four men in a convertible with simulated crosshairs on the head of the man sitting on the right-hand side back seat replicating JFK's seated position in the motorcade.

There are four pencil strokes across the automobile.

Below the photo are two rows of numbers and symbols, along with illegible notations, are written below the photo.

**26 - 14 - 28 - 14 - ' ' 1 / -** [illegible]
**42 - 24 - 64 - 72 - 1** [illegible]

**22**

**PAGE 22:**

At the top of this page, Roscoe wrote,

**trial doesn't surprise me**

The news-clipped photo is of Perry Raymond Russo, a key prosecution witness for New Orleans District Attorney Jim Garrison in the trial of Clay Shaw, a New Orleans businessman. Garrison charged Shaw with conspiracy in the assassination of President Kennedy. Russo testified that he was at a party where he overheard Shaw, a pilot named David Ferrie, and Lee Harvey Oswald discuss assassinating President Kennedy.

Roscoe wrote these words to the right of Russo's photo.

**Big mouth you talked after all**

Perry Raymond Russo died in 1995 at the age of 54.

Here, Roscoe admitted that he *knew* or *knew of* Russo's involvement with Shaw and Oswald as they discussed killing the president. He further knew that Russo had been warned to keep his mouth shut. Obviously, Russo didn't, and Roscoe called him *"a big mouth"* for "ratting on" the others.

At the bottom of this page are several illegible words.

**23**

**PAGE 23:**

This page shows news-clipped photos of two unidentified military men who appear to be wearing Vietnam-era uniforms. The presence of the two soldiers in the "scrapbook" may simply suggest that Roscoe knew or believed that one of the primary motives for Kennedy's assassination was his opposition to the Vietnam War. (Note: Kennedy's opposition to the Vietnam War directly conflicted with the advice and recommendations of his Joint Chiefs of Staff.)

## The Top Photo

Roscoe scribbled what appears to be someone's name above the top photo. However, it's indecipherable.

*Shoulder patch of the Army's 1st Aviation Brigade.*

The man in the top photo is wearing the shoulder patch of the Army's 1st Aviation Brigade and a Major General's two-star insignia on his collar. This brigade was the Army's largest aviation command, nearly equal in size to two divisions. The unit was organized in 1966, and in 1969, its headquarters was twenty-five miles northeast of Saigon.

The brigade's first Commander was Brigadier General George P. Seneff, Jr., who was later promoted to Major General. Seneff served as a Staff Aviation Officer at Military Assistance Command, Vietnam (MACV) from 1966 to 1967. (Note: <u>In 1963, General Seneff commanded the 11th Air Assault Aviation Group and developed air mobile tactics for Vietnam.)</u>

*Brigadier General George P. Seneff, Jr.*

As of this writing, there are two potential candidates for the identity of the military officer in the top photo.

One is Brigadier General George P. Seneff, Jr., and the other may be Major General Clifton F. von Kann. From July 1971 to September 1973, Brigadier General Seneff was assigned to the Army base at Ft. Hood, Texas. Ricky remembers reading in his father's diary about a burglary at this base. In the diary, Roscoe admitted his involvement in this burglary and wrote that one of the other men involved was accidentally killed. (Note: The diary entry described the removal of all identification from the dead man who was left at the scene.)

To the right of the scrapbook photos, there are several illegible notations.

Roscoe was killed two months after General Seneff arrived at Fort Hood in July 1971.

There are NO pencil marks on his photo.

Major General Clifton F. von Kann, another a leader of the 1st Aviation Brigade, is a second possible candidate for this unidentified soldier.

*Major General Clifton F. von Kann*

Major General von Kann, a 1937 Harvard graduate (MBA), became a leading figure in aviation. From 1951 to 1953, he worked in an executive capacity for the CIA. Later, he became Director of the U.S. Army's Aviation Department (1959-61); and from August 1963 to February 1965, he served as one of the commanding generals in Vietnam.

During the Nixon administration, Kann was recommended by Richard V. Allen, President Nixon's foreign policy advisor, for consideration as Deputy Director of the CIA.

In 1989, General Clifton von Kann became involved in a battle over control of Frances Knight Parrish's multimillion-dollar estate. Mrs. Parrish, known as "The Dragon Lady," was Director of the U.S. Passport Office from 1955 to 1977. Parrish was known as an outspoken, competent and tough administrator, who was often compared to her close friend, FBI Director J. Edgar Hoover.

Mrs. Knight Parrish "retired" in 1977 under controversial circumstances. This was during the time that the House Select Committee on Assassinations investigated the strange travels of Lee Harvey Oswald. (Note: The FBI discovered that someone was using Lee Harvey Oswald's passport while Oswald was still in Russia; a mystery that remains unresolved).

*Frances Knight Parrish*

**The Bottom Scrapbook Photo**

The bottom photo on this page appears to be from about the same time as the top photo.

In this clipping, Roscoe left a small portion of the photo's original caption that would have identified the soldier. The visible portion of the caption reads, "CAPT. RICK" or "CAPT. DICK."

There are <u>no</u> pencil marks on either photograph on this page.

The author's research led to the possibility that the soldier might be Captain Richard J. "Rick" Flaherty, a Captain in the Green Berets. As a Green Beret, he was awarded a Silver Star, two Bronze Stars, and two Purple Hearts. In 1971, he was "decommissioned" from the military (sheep dipped?) and entered the foggy world of a soldier of fortune. There, Flaherty gained a reputation for being a top-notch intelligence operative, caught the attention of the Central Intelligence Agency (CIA), and was recruited to run supplies, drugs, and weapons to countries in Central America. Later, after being abandoned by the CIA, Captain Flaherty infiltrated a smuggling ring at Fort Campbell, Kentucky. Additionally, he became an undercover operative for the Bureau of Alcohol, Tobacco, and Firearms (ATF).

In his last years, Rick became homeless and lived on the streets in Aventura, Florida.

In 2005, David Yuzuk, a military veteran, and Aventura, Florida police officer, befriended and offered to help Rick. Over time, Rick came to trust Yuzuk. Subsequently, he began sharing his life story, including time in the Green Berets, experiences as an undercover operative for the ATF, and work as a "soldier of fortune." Rick warned Officer Yuzuk that asking too many questions about him could be bad for his career and dangerous to his (Rick's) health.

On the night of May 9, 2015 – only eight hours after Officer Yuzuk made a call to confirm Rick's identity and background – Rick was struck by a motor vehicle while crossing a street in Aventura, Florida. He did not survive his injuries and was dead on arrival at the hospital.

Following his death, Yuzuk discovered that Rick had been issued several passports. Even though Rick appeared to be destitute and homeless, he traveled secretly to foreign countries such as Venezuela, Thailand, Vietnam, Iraq, and Jordan. Yuzuk was never able to determine how Rick afforded these trips. (Note: To learn more about Richard Flaherty, the reader is encouraged to read *The Giant Killer* by David A. Yuzuk with Neil L. Yuzuk. (Note: A video by the same title is also available on YouTube.)

(Note: Captain Flaherty's inclusion in the scrapbook may have meant that Roscoe recognized him, either by reputation or association.)

For comparison purposes, the photo on the left is "Rick" Flaherty while in Vietnam. The one on the right is Flaherty's high school graduation photo. The middle photo is a cropped version of the soldier in the scrapbook.

Below the bottom photo, Roscoe scribbled an indecipherable word, perhaps the person's name.

The authors want to be very clear here; these men are NOT accused of anything. Presently, their identities cannot be fully corroborated. If it is determined that these photos <u>are</u> of the above-named men, their only association may be having their photos in the scrapbook of an admitted assassin of President Kennedy.

**24**

**PAGE 24:**

Roscoe wrote a series of numbers at the top of this page.

**63 - 84 - 2 - 6**

The news-clipped photo is of a Dallas policeman and an unidentified civilian. These people appear to be using or examining hand-held radios in a retail store. The officer in the photo has been identified by another Dallas policeman as Joseph A. “Joe” Clark. The reason for this photo’s inclusion in the “scrapbook” is unknown.

There are three rows of illegible notations below the photo.

234 U DICTIONARY. VW

**PAGE 25:**

This is the final news-clipped photo found in Roscoe White's "scrapbook." It is taken from the front page of the March 18, 1967, edition of the *Dallas Times Herald.* The accompanying news story is about a two-year-old girl who was rescued alive and unharmed from a twenty-two-foot-deep well where she was trapped for nine hours. This incident is unrelated to Roscoe or the JFK assassination.

However, the lengthy article beside the photo is related; it pertains to New Orleans District Attorney Jim Garrison's prosecution of New Orleans businessman Clay Shaw for his alleged part in a conspiracy to assassinate President Kennedy. The main headline for this *Times Herald* edition is about the Vietnam War, while the paper's sub-headline reads: *"Way Cleared for Shaw Trial . . ."* The headline for the Shaw trial story reads: *"JFK Conspiracy Evidence Upheld."* The story briefly discusses the District Attorney's "*victory*" following a four-day preliminary hearing where he produced *"two major witnesses, Perry R. Russo and Vernon Bundy."* This meant that the evidence presented in the hearing was sufficient for the State of Louisiana to try Shaw on conspiracy charges related to the assassination.

Did Roscoe place this news article in the "scrapbook" to call additional attention to Shaw's importance and prosecution related to JFK's assassination? Was Roscoe saying that the trial was a key connection to what took place in Dallas on November 22nd? The authors believe the answer to this question is a strong yes!

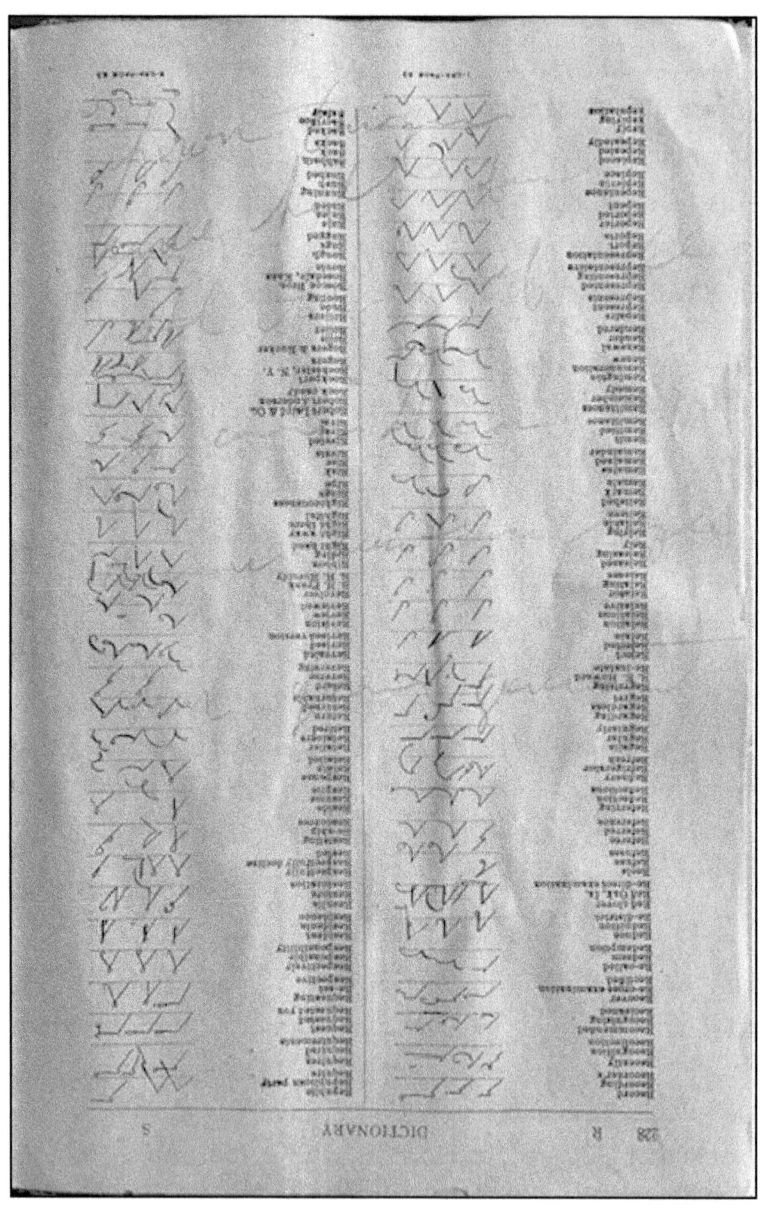

**26**

**PAGE 26:**

There are no news clippings on this page; only six lines of handwritten notations. Unfortunately, these notations have mostly faded away, thereby rendering them almost impossible to read or understand.

As best as could be deciphered, Roscoe wrote the following six lines.

***from triumvir***
***came hell for***
***all the grief all***
***to cause America***
***curse went over life***
***from your government***

In this strangely worded, poetry-like notation, Roscoe appeared to be telling us that "*hell*" came from this "*triumvir*," caused "*grief*" to "*America*," a "*curse*" over "*life*," and it all originated with "*your government*" and NOT from some foreign entity.

The term "triumvir" was a term that was not in common use during the 1960s; it refers to *"Government by three persons who share authority and responsibility."*

The meaning of these words and the identities of the three persons of the *"triumvir"* remains a mystery; perhaps it all served as some type of coded message.

Inside the front dust jacket of *The Improbable Triumvirate, Kennedy – Khrushchev – Pope John, An Asterisk to the History of a Hopeful Year, 1962-1963,* a 1972 book written by Norman Cousins, are these words:

> *The book tells of some remarkable exchanges between Pope John and Premier Khrushchev. It was the Pope who took the initiative in establishing direct contacts between the Vatican and the Kremlin. A specific result of this was the release, after years of interment of two archbishops. Mr. Cousins was chosen as an emissary of the Vatican to negotiate the release. During this time, President Kennedy asked Mr. Cousins to play a role In the preliminary negotiations for an agreement to halt the testing of nuclear weapons. The book deals with the role of public opinion in making the nuclear test-ban treaty possible. As an outgrowth of the experiences related here, Mr. Cousins was asked by the President to work on the campaign for ratification of the treaty. This book provides an account of that work."*

Roscoe's use of the word "triumvir" suggests that he may have had some knowledge of the negotiations that transpired in 1962-1963 between the Pope, Khrushchev, and Kennedy. (Note: These negotiations are outlined in Cousin's book.)

Another possibility is what David Schieim labeled as "the Mob's anti-Kennedy triumvirate," meaning Florida chieftain Santos Trafficante, New Orleans mafia chieftain Carlos

Marcello and American labor union head Jimmy Hoffa. All three had connections to Jack Ruby, and thus to Roscoe White. (Schieim, David; *Contract on America*, p. 159-160)

Or might the triumvir have been the military, industrial, and intelligence conglomerate that was so at odds with Kennedy at the time.

Q. Do you know whether or not this railroad company received and discharged passengers at the stopping place at the crossing?

Objected to by counsel for defendant as irrelevant and immaterial. Overruled. To which ruling the defendant by its counsel, then and there, duly excepted at the time.

A. They are not supposed to receive and discharge passengers there. If a man gets on or off there, he does so entirely on his own risk.

Q. Do you know whether the company receive and discharge them there? A. They are not supposed to.

Q. Do you know whether they do that or not? A. I don't know, I am hardly ever down there; my station, you know, is at the depot.

CROSS EXAMINATION.

By Mr. Hamlin—

Q. I understand you to say that it is positively against the instructions to the agents to sell tickets on any train that does not stop at the stations? A. Yes, sir.

Q. A man can come and buy a ticket to-day, and ride on it at any time when he can catch a train? A. Yes, sir.

Q. When they are sold, they are not sold with the understanding that the purchaser is to ride on trains that do not stop at the station, where it is sold? A. No, sir.

Q. It is a fact that an agent would be fired if he should authorize or attempt to authorize a person to get on a train that didn't stop there? A. Yes, sir; those are the rules of the company.

---

E. W. Kells, sworn and examined as a witness on the part of the plaintiffs, testified as follows:

DIRECT EXAMINATION.

By Mr. Timmonds—

Q. Where do you reside? A. At Fort Scott, Kans.

Q. What is your business? A. I am a locomotive engineer.

Q. For what company? A. The K. C. F. S. & M.

Q. How long have you been employed by that company? A. Almost ten years, it will be in a month or two.

Q. Where do you run now? A. I am running between Kansas City and Springfield.

Q. How long have you been a locomotive engineer? A. I commenced my first running in 1873; that is, to go any distance on the road; I had been handling an engine before that.

Q. How old are you? A. Fifty-one past.

Q. Did you as an engineer have control of an engine pulling freight train No. 48 over this railroad through this county, on the night of the 24th of December last? A. Yes, sir.

Q. Were you on time or behind time? A. I was behind time.

Q. About how much behind time? A. I don't just recollect, but I presume I was a couple of hours behind time.

**PAGE 27:**

There are no news clippings on this page, but along the right margin, Roscoe wrote what appears to be the following mathematical equation.

**20-**
**—--------** divided into **7**
**60-**

The meaning of this notation is unknown.

**CLOSING THOUGHTS:**

There was an unusual incident that Ricky and Tricia thought might have been related to their possession of the "scrapbook." On August 4, 1990, while returning home after meeting with Oliver Stone in Los Angeles, the Delta Airlines flight Ricky and Tricia were aboard made an emergency landing at an isolated runway at the Dallas/Fort Worth airport. Delta's Los Angeles reservation office had received a report of a bomb threat. As the plane was about to land, the flight crew instructed the passengers that once the plane came to a stop, they were to immediately exit the plane. They were directed *not* to take anything from the plane, which included any items stored in the overhead compartments. (Note: Tricia had packed the green "scrapbook" inside her carry-on bag that was stored in the overhead compartment.) When the plane came to a stop, Tricia quickly retrieved the book from the overhead compartment, placed it in her camera bag, and exited the plane by way of the emergency slides.

Ricky and Tricia said as they got away from the plane, they immediately noticed there were no fire trucks or emergency equipment nearby. However, they did see numerous unmarked cars and men in dark suits boarding the plane as they stood on the tarmac. After nearly an hour, shuttle buses arrived and transported the passengers to the nearest terminal. Several weeks after the event, Ricky and Tricia received their luggage from the airline and it was obvious their bags had been thoroughly searched.

The Whites never learned the reason for this strange and upsetting emergency. That they were extremely unnerved by it is certainly understandable.

How important is this “scrapbook?” We believe it is very important.

METRO SCENE

# 13 passengers hurt at DFW in bomb scare

A Delta jet en route to Dallas from Los Angeles was forced to evacuate Friday at Dallas-Fort Worth International Airport after a phony bomb threat was reported.

At least 13 of the jet's 230 passengers suffered minor injuries when the plane landed at 3:45 p.m. Passengers complained that three emergency chutes did not unfold.

A bomb threat was called into Delta's Los Angeles reservations office soon before the Boeing jet was to land and then head to Atlanta, said Joe Licitra, a Delta spokesman.

FBI agents, DFW Department of Public Safety officers and bomb squad dogs searched for explosive devices, but found none, an airport spokesman said.

After landing, passengers and 11 crew members slid down emergency chutes.

"Two of the slides over the wing didn't open [until] we were all away from the plane," said Richard Potapow, 44, of Bel Air, Calif.

Charles Reynolds, 54, of Haughton, La., who had been asked by a flight attendant to help open a rear emergency exit, said there was no emergency slide.

Boeing officials in Seattle said they were unaware of the incident and had no comment.

*Dallas Morning News, August 4, 1990*

Admittedly, neither Ricky nor the co-authors completely understand Roscoe's intentions and meanings for his "scrapbook." That being said, we have attempted – to the very best of our ability – to decipher, understand, and describe many of the news clippings and scribbled notations. Furthermore, we have identified people in various photos and hypothesized about others. The number sequences, symbols, and scribblings throughout the scrapbook are well "above our pay grade" and beyond our interpretive capabilities. However, there is a possibility, maybe even probability, that they, in totality, hold a key or keys to a fuller understanding of what Roscoe wanted us to know.

Please help if you can.

***". . . the solution to the perplexing and exasperating question as to who ordered and carried out the assassination of President Kennedy will never be found in any government documents. If such documentation ever existed within this government's files and/or archives, they were undoubtedly destroyed long ago."***

***— J. Gary Shaw***

# CHAPTER SEVEN: Believe It or Don't

In an article entitled, *"I Was Mandarin..."* published in the December 1990 issue of *Texas Monthly* magazine, highly respected journalist and author, Gary Cartwright wrote these thought-provoking words:

> *"I don't know what happened back in November 1963, but you'll have to sell the lone nut theory somewhere else... If the entire Roscoe White story is a hoax — and that is a distinct possibility — it is a hoax created by someone with an impressive knowledge of assassination details, a good grasp of intelligence operations, and some insight into organized crime."*

The authors strongly agree. So, why should anyone believe the Roscoe White revelations?

The reasons that the story has merit and is worthy of consideration and belief are many and multifaceted.

**Believe It Because....**

– <u>Because</u>, first and foremost, the discovery of the metal canister that contained the three *"Navy Int"* messages, and the green "scrapbook" that revealed information confirming what Ricky previously read in his father's stolen diary; namely, that Roscoe admitted his participation in the assassination. This discovery occurred about five years <u>after</u> Ricky first read the diary.

– <u>Because</u> Roscoe White's story offers a far more plausible and realistic explanation for what happened than that of the outrageous "lone nut" and "lone avenger" fabrication proffered in each of the so-called investigations by the official authorities. And we – the authors – believe that the story is accompanied by a more persuasive narrative and supporting documentation.

– <u>Because</u> of the honesty and integrity of Ricky and Tricia White. They are honest, hard-working, and family-oriented people. Deceitfulness is not in either of them. They simply were — and remain — totally incapable of devising and creating such a complicated array of scenarios and artifacts.

– <u>Because</u> of how we were made aware of the story. None of the original five recipients of Ricky White's story sought, nor expected such a surprising and utterly believable revelation, accompanied by considerable evidentiary material and additional clues that warranted further investigation and research.

– <u>Because</u> of the amazingly swift and fierce way the story was attacked by government officials, the media, and the lone-nut crowd, who considered it just another JFK assassination "conspiracy theory" and hoax. Without question, there was a ruthless and desperate attack on Ricky and his story; and, rather than investigate, these powerful and influential entities quickly expressed their distaste and attempted to repudiate the story.

Here are just a few of their blatantly oblivious comments:

> David Belin, who served as staff counsel on two government investigations of the Kennedy assassination, is quoted in the *Dallas Times Herald* as saying: "*It's a fairytale. And it's a fairytale that's an outgrowth of hallucinatory drugs*." Belin's smug declaration came with absolutely no firsthand knowledge of the complete story.
>
> The *Chicago Tribune printed that CIA spokesman, Mark Mansfield* said: "*Bobby Inman, a former naval intelligence director and CIA deputy director, said the cables appeared to be a 'forgery of some kind.'*" Of course, Inman never saw the cables.
>
> Additionally, the *Tribune* quoted the CIA, who "*... called White's allegations ludicrous. This individual who is mentioned, Roscoe White, was never employed by the CIA or associated in anyway with the agency, CIA spokesman, Mark Mansfield said. "We normally never confirm or deny employment, but these allegations are so outrageous that we felt it was necessary and appropriate to respond.*" And

> this from an agency that has always told us the truth — we think not!
>
> A *Dallas Times Herald* article quoted G. Robert Blakey, Chief Counsel and Staff Director to the U.S. House Select Committee on Assassinations: *"This sort of thing occurs about every two or three months and has done so for about 20 years. Even if this is the truth, I probably won't believe it because at this stage of the history of the assassination virtually anyone can fabricate a story by going to the* [historical] *record. In a sense, it's too late to confess and be believable."*

These quotes were published the following day <u>before</u> any attempt to address or investigate Ricky's allegations.

– <u>Because</u> of the provenance and authenticity of the material and artifacts provided to the authors.

> *"John Stockwell, former chief of the Central Intelligence Agency's Angola Task Force in Washington, D.C., has seen the messages and sees a '90 to 95 percent probability that they are genuine.'"*
>
> *"Office of Naval Intelligence spokesman John Wanat says the agency cannot determine whether the messages came from authentic ONI cables without the coded cables. 'What they have there is really nothing that we can narrow down as far as who may have generated it or if it's legitimate or whether it's*

> *something that was fabricated,' Wanat said after viewing texts of the messages."*

– Because of the conspicuous agitation and uneasiness displayed by FBI personnel before their seeing, reading, and photocopying the diary. Why did they initiate unwarranted surveillance of Ricky and Tricia White? The agents had only heard about the Roscoe White diary and its contents from the Midland County Assistant District Attorney, Al Schorre. What did the FBI hope to gain from the surveillance of two innocent citizens?

It was not until January 13, 1988, a full two weeks after FBI agents began their unjustified surveillance, that they finally approached Ricky at his home. The agents frightened him and warned him of possible fines and imprisonment if he failed to cooperate; then, they ordered him to bring his father's material to their offices for examination. Then, wrote a false and misleading report about what transpired.

While Ricky was with the agents, they interrogated and intimidated him while a United States Senator in Washington listened in on a speakerphone. Ricky is convinced this "third party" was Pennsylvania Senator Arlen Specter; the same senator who created and promoted the ridiculous single bullet theory to the world. These bullying tactics are especially significant given the FBI's well-documented interference and dishonesty relating to many of the other witnesses connected to the Kennedy case, those whose testimony was considered out of line with the government's predetermined lone-nut scenario.

– Because White and Oswald were in the Marine Corps at the same time, sailed together to the Far East on the same ship, and were stationed in the same locale for three months.

– Because both men are pictured together in the same overseas snapshot. This photo was in Roscoe's possession when his assassination-related material was discovered.

– Because Roscoe began working for the Dallas Police at about the same time Lee Oswald began his employment with the Texas School Book Depository.

– Because Roscoe, who was well acquainted with Jack Ruby, arranged for his wife to work as a hostess at his clubs. (Note: See photo of Geneva and Ruby.)

– Because multiple witnesses also reported a close association between Jack Ruby and Lee Oswald – an association that governmental officials lied about and denied.

**Did Roscoe White Do It?**

Did Roscoe White play a major role in the assassination of President Kennedy?

He admitted that he did — in his own handwriting.

Ricky believes he did, and that his father left behind supporting material of his guilt for Ricky to discover, disclose, and possibly shed additional light on the darkness that still surrounds the politically and financially motivated murder of the president.

The authors believe that there is a very high probability that Roscoe did play a major role in the assassination and have spent thousands of hours researching and investigating this very complex story.

Despite the official lone-gunman verdict, there is overwhelming evidence that a gunman fired at President Kennedy from behind the stockade fence on the grassy knoll — the very location from which Roscoe White admitted he shot.

**Proof of a shot from the Front**

Author/researcher Stewart Galanor carefully listed many of the assassination witnesses and noted that 216 stated their opinion as to the origin of the shot or shots fired at JFK. Of these 216 witnesses: 52 said a shot or shots came from the knoll; 48 said from the Texas School Book Depository; 5 said from both the knoll and the Depository; 4 said from elsewhere; 37 were unsure and 70 were not asked.

Adding to this compelling number of 57 corroborating witnesses who believed that a shot or shots came from the grassy knoll area is the fact that 21 of these 57 were law enforcement officers who possessed more than average experience with gunfire.

The Warren Commission, in cover-up mode, elected to acknowledge and promote *only* those 48 witnesses who said that the shots came from the Depository and ignored and/or rejected the 57 witnesses who reported that shots came from the grassy knoll.

In addition to the lawmen and others who immediately rushed towards the grassy knoll area, there were:

– Witnesses who had observed men standing behind the stockade fence before the motorcade's arrival in Dealey Plaza.

– Witnesses who found cigarette butts along with "hundreds" of footprints in the mud along the north side of the stockade fence -- as if someone had been pacing back and forth awaiting the arrival of the motorcade.

– Witnesses who, at the time of the shooting, saw a "flash" or something out of the ordinary that called their attention to the area of the stockade fence.

– Witnesses who, as shots were fired, saw a "puff of smoke" coming from the area of the stockade fence.

– Witnesses who saw a man with a rifle in the area beyond the stockade fence.

– Witnesses who heard gunfire coming from the stockade fence area.

– Witnesses who saw President Kennedy's head being thrown violently backward as he was struck by the fatal headshot; indicating beyond <u>reasonable</u> doubt that the source of the bullet was fired from a location in front of the President.

– Parkland hospital doctors attending the stricken President saw an entrance wound in the <u>front</u> of the

President's neck, a wound that could only have been caused by a bullet fired from the front.

– Several Parkland doctors noted a large gaping wound in the back of the President's head they believed was an exit wound further suggesting a shot originated from the grassy knoll.

– Witnesses who observed a portion of the President's skull blown backward and landing on the trunk of the limousine.

– Witnesses who saw blood and brain matter travel through the air and strike the face and helmet of one of the police motorcycle escorts riding just to the left and behind the Presidential limousine, indicative of a shot from the grassy knoll area.

– A witness who saw an unidentified man with "*something in his right hand*" run north away from the picket fence immediately after the shots.

– A witness who stood on the south side of Elm Street about whom the FBI noted and wrote about in one of their early reports:

> *"One of the 35 mm color slides depicted a female wearing a brown coat taking pictures from an angle, which would have, undoubtedly, included the Texas School Book Depository in the background of her pictures. Her pictures evidently were taken just as the President was shot."*

What is <u>not</u> noted in this report is that from the woman's position her pictures, "*...taken just as the President was shot,"* would have undoubtedly captured, not only all the activity in and around the grassy knoll and picket fence area but also the sixth-floor window from which Oswald allegedly fired as well.

Unfortunately, the woman's undeveloped film was confiscated by a man identifying himself as an FBI agent and never returned. What is certain, however, is that if the "pictures" had shown only Oswald in the window at the time of the shooting they would have been displayed and ballyhooed to the entire universe.

Taken together, the observations of these eye and ear witnesses establish an extremely high probability — even certainty — that a shot or shots were fired at the President from his right front, the direction of the "grassy knoll." This is the same location from which Roscoe White admitted he fired; and, the government's absurd <u>lone assassin</u>, single bullet theory is a bald-faced lie!

**The Verdict Belongs to YOU!**

With these things in mind, does the Roscoe White story have merit? Could the story be true?

Investigative reporter Gary Cartwright may have said it best when he wrote:

> "*If the Roscoe White story was a hoax, I decided early on, Ricky was its victim, not its perpetrator. <u>He no more could have invented or even acted out a</u>*

> *hoax of this sophistication than he could have explained the universe."* (emphasis ours).

Is the Roscoe White story just another elaborate hoax analogous to the Warren Report and other nonsensical governmental "lone assassin" proclamations?

Admittedly, it might be. The authors don't believe it is, but as was urged at the beginning of this book, that should be YOUR call.

Ask yourself: if it were not true, why would anyone, especially a family-loving man like Roscoe, leave behind such a devastating legacy? And why would his son, also a family-loving man, put himself and his family through such a painful ordeal?

In the minds of many, President Kennedy's violent murder was a coup d'état that caused great damage to this country and its people; and the deliberate "official" lies and obvious cover-ups regarding his assassination have continued to exponentially compound that unrelenting harm.

The truth about President Kennedy's murder will never come from our government — but maybe the Roscoe White story can point us in a direction that helps find it.

Hopefully, it's a start.

# APPENDIX A

## Roscoe White Story Timeline: 1935-2023

**March 25, 1911**
Jack Ruby was born in Chicago, Illinois.

**November 18, 1935**
Roscoe Anthony White was born in Glenwood, Arkansas to Lydia "Merle" Harrington and Joseph White. While Roscoe was still an infant, his father abandoned the family and was never seen again. Merle and Roscoe moved to Cloverdale, Indiana to live with her parents, James Walton and Florence May Harrington.

**June 14, 1941**
Geneva Ruth Toland was born to Mary and Weldon Toland in Paris, Texas. Geneva was the youngest and last of nine children born to the Toland family.

**Circa 1947**
Jack Ruby moved from Chicago to Dallas.

**Circa 1948**
Roscoe turned thirteen years old while living with his maternal grandparents in Foreman, Arkansas.

**April 7, 1950**
According to the 1950 U.S. Census, Roscoe and his mother lived in Foreman, Arkansas with his mother Lida "Merle" Harrington's parents.

**May 21, 1954**
After graduating from Foreman High School, Roscoe

rejoined his mother and new stepfather, Daniel Boone Rogers in Paris, Texas.

**Spring 1956**

Twenty-one-year-old Roscoe White met and began dating fifteen-year-old Geneva Ruth Toland.

**May 8, 1956**

Roscoe began employment with Convair Corporation, a division of General Dynamics in Fort Worth, Texas.

**July 28, 1956**

Roscoe resigned from Convair Corporation. During Roscoe's brief employment with the company, John Mason Lankford was the Director of Security. It was Lankford who later verified Roscoe's employment with the Dallas Police Department.

At the time of the assassination, Lankford was with the Fort Worth branch of the Office of Naval Intelligence, often referred to as "Navy Int." or ONI. He was also Fort Worth's Fire Marshall, who was recruited by James M. "Mike" Howard of the Secret Service to provide firemen as security while President and Mrs. Kennedy stayed at Fort Worth's Texas Hotel the night before the assassination. The Secret Service agents assigned to the President's detail left their posts and went to The Cellar, a nearby Fort Worth nightclub run by Jack Ruby's friend, Pat Kirkwood. Several agents assigned to the motorcade were observed drinking in the club past midnight.

**November 11, 1956**
Due to her age (15), Geneva and Roscoe eloped and were married in a civil ceremony in Hugo, Oklahoma.

**February 19, 1957**
Roscoe and Geneva's brother Benjamin enlisted in the United States Marine Corps in Dallas.

**August 21, 1957**
Roscoe White shipped out from San Diego aboard the *USS Bexar* headed for Japan. Another Marine from Texas, Lee Harvey Oswald, was also on the ship.

**May 1, 1959**
Roscoe reenlisted in the Marines for another six years. Reenlistment pushed back his discharge date to December 1963.

**August 10, 1959**
Geneva gave birth to her first child, Roscoe Anthony "Tony" White, Jr.

**Winter 1959**
Jack Ruby became a partner with Joe Slatin in The Sovereign Club at 1312 1⁄2 Commerce Street. (Note: Later, Ruby changed the club's name to The Carousel Club).

**November 24, 1960**
Roscoe's second child, Ricky Don White was born.

**August 5, 1962**
Dallas County real estate records show Roscoe and Geneva purchased the home at 1226 North Morocco. At the time

Geneva worked as a waitress at The Cattleman's Steakhouse in Fort Worth.

**November 13, 1962**
Roscoe submitted a request for a hardship discharge from the Marine Corps.

**November 27, 1962**
Roscoe was transferred to the Naval Air Station in Dallas while awaiting his discharge.

**December 4, 1962**
Roscoe was honorably discharged from the Marine Corps and subsequently no longer obligated to serve his remaining time in the Reserves.

**December 7, 1962**
Roscoe began work full-time as an insurance agent with American National Insurance Company in Dallas.

**December 12, 1962**
Roscoe applied for a position with the Dallas Police Department, and a background check was initiated (Note: Roscoe's application is not in his personnel file.)

**February 1963**
Roscoe received the first of three plain-text messages from "Navy Int." This message stated:

> *"Forgein [sic] Affairs assignments have been canceled. The next assignment is to eliminate a National Security threat to worldwide peace. Destination will be Houston, Austin, or Dallas.*

> *Contacts are being arranged now. Orders are subject to change at any time. Reply back if not understood."*

**August 13, 1963**
Roscoe began work as a part-time insurance agent with Farmers Insurance Company in Dallas.

**September 1963 (3 events)**
**1)** Roscoe began working weekends as a freight handler with Roadway Express Company in Dallas.

**2)** Roscoe received a second plain-text message from "Navy Int." stating:

> *"Dallas destination chosen. Your place hidden within the department. Contacts are within this letter. continue on as planned."*

**3)** Geneva quit her job at The Cattleman's Steakhouse, and Roscoe arranged for her to work as a hostess at Jack Ruby's club(s).

**September 25, 1963**
Roscoe White's pre-employment background investigation was completed and forwarded to Dallas Police Chief Curry for final approval.

**October 7, 1963**
Roscoe was hired as an apprentice policeman with the Dallas Police Department. His starting monthly salary was $370. He attended the next police academy in December.

**October 18, 1963**

Lee Harvey Oswald began working at the Texas School Book Depository.

**November 1963**

One afternoon while at the Carousel Club, Geneva overheard Roscoe and Jack Ruby discussing the assassination of President Kennedy. Ruby threatened to have Geneva killed if she revealed what she heard. Roscoe told Ruby that he would arrange for Geneva to have electro-shock treatments to erase her memory. Geneva overheard Roscoe tell Ruby, "*We can go ahead, I have a guy that I know, he's a Mason, I can get him to give Geneva shock treatments.*"

**November 8, 1963**

Lee Harvey Oswald wrote a letter to someone named Hunt in which he requested clarification *"concerding* [sic] *my position."* The purpose of this letter is unclear.

**November 22, 1963**

President John Kennedy was assassinated while riding in a motorcade in Dealey Plaza. Dallas Police Motorcycle Officer Bobby Hargis, flanking the left side of the President's limo, charged up the knoll immediately after the shooting and encountered Roscoe White in uniform near the picket fence (Note: See timeline entry for July 1, 2003.)

Eyewitness Beverly Oliver, standing on the south side of Elm Street, saw Roscoe on the grassy knoll immediately after the shots. She said Roscoe was not wearing a hat or gun belt.

Dallas Police Officer J. D. Tippit was shot and killed. Lee Harvey Oswald was arrested at the Texas Theater.

**November 24, 1963**
Despite being surrounded by numerous law enforcement personnel, Lee Harvey Oswald was shot in the basement of the Dallas police station while being transferred to the county jail. The assassin's "assassin" was Jack Ruby – a nightclub owner, an FBI informant, Roscoe White's friend, and at one time Roscoe's wife's employer.

**November 25, 1963**
Lee Oswald was buried at Rose Hill Cemetery in Fort Worth.

**December 4, 1963**
Roscoe began recruit training at the Dallas Police Academy.

**December 1963**
Roscoe received the third plain-text message from "Navy Int." directing him to:

> *"Stay within the* [police] *department, witnesses have eyes, ears, and mouths. You know what to do about the mix-up. The men will be in to cover up all misleading evidence soon. Stay as planned, wait for further orders."*

**Circa January 1964**
Geneva was admitted to Sherman Veteran's Hospital in Sherman, Texas, and administered the first of many electro-shock treatments throughout her life.

**February 28, 1964**
Roscoe graduated from the police academy.

**March 14, 1964**
Jack Ruby was convicted of murder with malice aforethought and sentenced to death.

**June 1965**
Marina Oswald married Kenneth Porter in Fate, Texas. Porter was working at Texas Instruments at the time.

**October 17, 1965**
Roscoe resigned from the police department; he wrote the following in his resignation letter to the Chief of Police: *"I have accepted employment with Page's Drug Store beginning October 18, 1965."*

**May 3, 1966**
Dallas County property records indicated that the Whites sold their home at 1226 North Morocco.

**June 8, 1966**
Dallas County property records indicated that Roscoe and Geneva purchased a home at 219 Glencarin Drive. (Note: The White's new home was 300 feet east of Marie Tippit's residence at 238 Glencarin Drive.)

**October 27, 1966**
Roscoe White executed his last will and testament in the offices of prominent Dallas criminal defense attorney Lamar Holley, close associate of Lyndon Johnson in the 1950s. Coincidentally, Holley served as Johnson's campaign manager.

**November 22, 1966**
Medical records obtained by Ricky indicated that his mother received additional electro-shock treatments beginning on November 22, 1966. From 1966 to 1971, Geneva received twenty-six shock treatments while under the care of Dr. Daniel B. Pearson.

**December 19, 1966**
Jack Ruby was admitted to Parkland Hospital with pneumonia.

**January 3, 1967**
Jack Ruby died at Parkland Hospital. The results of autopsy indicated that the cause of death was due to, *"Complications due to cancer."* (Note: There was a blood clot inside a blood vessel of the heart.)

**March 13, 1967**
Dallas County real estate records indicated that Roscoe and Geneva sold the home at 219 Glencairn.

**March to August 1967**
The family moved to Mountain Home, Arkansas to live with Roscoe's widowed maternal grandfather. At that time, Ricky and Geneva believed that Roscoe worked for the local post office, but no employment record has been found to confirm this.

**September 1967**
The White family returned to Dallas and moved into an apartment in the Kingswood Apartment complex on Kings Road. Roscoe and Geneva began working for M.E. Moses Company, a small "five and dime" variety store in Dallas.

This was where Roscoe and Geneva first met Reverend Jack Shaw. Ricky remembers this was when his father began wearing a toupee full-time.

**Circa 1969**

Roscoe began working for M & M Equipment and Rental Company on Ferguson Road in Dallas. The company repaired heavy construction machinery. Roscoe was eventually promoted to shop foreman and welder. According to the FBI, Dan Rasmussen, the owner of the business, took out a $300,000 insurance policy on Roscoe.

**April 7, 1969**

Dallas County real estate records indicated that the Whites purchased the home at 727 Nottingham in Richardson. (Note:At this time, Marina Oswald and Ken Porter rented a house two blocks north of the Whites. Additionally, Marina's youngest daughter, Rachel, attended the same 4th-grade class with Ricky White at Richardson Heights Elementary School.

**Spring 1971 (2 events)**

During one visit to their cabin at Lake Whitney, Texas, Ricky remembers watching his father spend most of one day digging a hole at the property and burying a metal box. He estimated the box to be 12" tall by 7" wide. The box has never been found.

Geneva sold Viviane Woodard Cosmetics to earn extra money and won a trip to New Orleans based on her sales record. She asked her husband to accompany her but he refused.

One evening, while she and other attendees were at a New Orleans nightclub, Geneva was approached by a stranger who introduced himself as “Nick” and told her that he knew her husband. They moved to another table where “Nick” threatened to harm her and her children unless Roscoe contacted him within 48 hours. Geneva returned home immediately and told Roscoe about the threat.

Finally, Roscoe told Geneva about his involvement in the assassination.

**Late Spring 1971**
Roscoe applied for a position as a police officer with the city of Forney, Texas, twenty miles east of Dallas.

**June 23, 1971**
Roscoe sold his interest in the Lake Whitney cabin to his brother-in-law.

**September 23, 1971**
Roscoe White and fellow employee Dick Adair are seriously injured in an explosion and fire at M & M Equipment and Rental Company in Dallas. Before Roscoe died, he confessed to his minister that he had “. . . *sinned against his country and taken lives on foreign and domestic soil.*”

**September 24, 1971**
Geneva asked their attorney Lamar Holley to represent her in settling her husband’s estate.

**September 27, 1971**
Roscoe Anthony White is buried with full military honors and laid to rest in the Field of Honor at Restland Memorial

Park in Dallas. The ceremony is conducted by both military and Masonic personnel and Ricky believes that it was at this time that he was introduced to "Colonel Bond" during the service.

**December 7, 1971**

Geneva sold the house at 727 Nottingham; she and her sons moved back to Paris, Texas.

**December 15, 1972**

Attorney Lamar Holley probated Roscoe White's last will and testament on behalf of Geneva.

**Circa 1973**

Dick Adair and Geneva filed a joint lawsuit against Arrow Chemical Corporation, manufacturers of the highly flammable and corrosive chemical HC-68 that caused the injuries to Adair and White. The chemical company denied all responsibility for the explosion and the case was settled out of court. The White family was awarded $40,000. In an interview with Andy Burke several years later, Adair said he believed the explosion was suspicious.

**August 4, 1973**

Geneva married Ben Kirtland Dees in Lamar, Texas, and purchased the home at 3405 Bonham Street, Paris, Texas.

**February 1, 1974**

While alone at her home, Geneva claimed that two men forcibly entered and assaulted her. She told the police that one of the suspects struck her on the head, rendering her unconscious.

She also claimed that the two men stole her husband's assassination-related material. (Note: The police report did not indicate that Geneva suffered any injuries, only that a small amount of jewelry was taken.) No suspects were ever identified.

**February 18, 1974**

Dr. Donald Offutt admitted Geneva to Timberlawn Psychiatric Hospital in Dallas where she remained hospitalized for two months.

**January 17, 1975**

Roscoe's mother, Lydia "Merle" Harrington married Daniel Boone Rogers in Johnson City, Texas.

**March 6, 1975**

Robert Groden and comedian Dick Gregory appeared on *Good Night America;* the ABC late-night television show hosted by Geraldo Rivera. Groden and Gregory showed the Zapruder film for the first time on national television. The public's response to the film led to the formation of the Hart-Schweicker investigation, which contributed to the Church Committee investigation on Intelligence Activities and subsequently resulted in the formation of the House Select Committee on Assassinations.

**Circa 1975**

The United States Senate established a committee to investigate suspected abuses of power by the US intelligence community. Headed by Frank Church (D-Idaho), the committee's findings eventually led to the establishment of a permanent Senate Select Committee on Intelligence to oversee intelligence activities. This committee passed the Foreign Intelligence Surveillance Act.

**March 1975**

Geneva contacted Dallas criminal defense Attorney Lamar Holley to discuss money owed her from the trust fund set up by her late husband. She told Holley about the photographs her husband procured while he was employed with the police department and of her desire to sell them. Geneva gave the photos to Holley and was given a receipt.

**July 1975**

Geneva was introduced to three men who claimed to be related to her present husband, Ben Dees. The men convinced her they could sell all the assassination-related photos for one million dollars. After retrieving the photos from Holly, Geneva drove to Arkansas and gave the photos to two of the men. Later, Geneva received a worthless check for the photos; subsequently, she contacted the FBI. Eventually, the FBI arrested all three men in Arizona, and the photos were recovered.

Geneva contacted Gerald Weatherly of the Dallas County District Attorney's Office; she requested his assistance in recovering the set of 34 photographs taken from her under false pretenses. Geneva informed Weatherly that the photos proved that Lee Oswald was connected to the Central Intelligence Agency. Geneva submitted a sworn affidavit in support of her complaint.

Weatherly believed Geneva's story and referred her to the Dallas County Texas Grand Jury for assistance. A date for the grand jury hearing had not been finalized when Weatherly wrote an undated letter to Senator Richard Schweicker, Congressman Henry Gonzalez, and Texas Attorney General Waggoner Carr suggesting that the Kennedy assassination investigation should be reopened. Weatherly stated in the letter that he planned to call Geneva as a witness and issue a subpoena requiring the defendant, Dan Robinson, to appear before the grand jury.

The FBI kept the photographs and turned them over to the Senate's Schweiker-Hart Committee. In January 1976, the committee returned the photographs to Geneva. Later, Ricky turned over a wooden rifle stock belonging to his father to Jonathan Blackmer of the HSCA.

**August 22, 1975**
A Dallas District Attorney's case summary stated that 34 photographs had been taken from Geneva White under false pretenses. The three men involved were Dan Robinson and brothers Deft and Pat Logan.

**September 29, 1975**
Weatherly wrote a second letter to Schweicker, Gonzalez, and Waggoner Carr informing them of a phone call to Geneva regarding the grand jury referral. She told Weatherly:

> *"The pictures were left to her by her deceased former husband, Roscoe A. White, and that he was on the Police Force of the City of Dallas, Texas, two years - what branch is unknown to her."*

Weatherly wrote that he contacted the DPD's personnel department which verified Roscoe's employment from a card in his file. Roscoe joined the department on October 7, 1963, and resigned on October 18, 1965; however, there was no information in his personnel file identifying what division he was assigned while he was with the department.

**March 1976**

Geneva received a call from Don Marston of the Schweicker Committee who had been contacted by a reporter for *New Times* magazine. The reporter wanted to purchase a copy of the third backyard photo. Geneva sold a copy for $500, and the photo was published in the magazine's April edition.

**September 1976**

The United States House of Representatives passed House Resolution 1540 establishing the House Select Committee on Assassinations (HSCA) in Washington, D.C. The committee subpoenaed Dallas mob boss Joseph Campisi to appear before the committee. Campisi retained Lamar Holley to represent him.

**November 1976**

Without legal representation, Geneva appeared before a panel of inquiry at the request of the Dallas District Attorney's office.

**December 30-31, 1976**

House Select Committee Assassination investigators Jon Blackmer and Kevin Walsh travel to Paris, Texas and interview Geneva and Ricky. At the conclusion of the 2-day interview, Geneva allowed the investigators to take 42 assassination-related material obtained by Roscoe while he was with the Dallas Police Department. Believing that Roscoe may have placed a microdot on a rifle stock, Ricky allowed Blackmer to take the rifle back to Washington for analysis.

**January 6, 1977**

The HSCA memo below summarized the Schweiker Committee's and the HSCA's investigation into the Roscoe White materials:

> *"From: HSCA memo Blackmer to Tanenbaum dated January 6, 1977.*
>
> *Chain of custody of the evidence received from Mrs. Geneva Dees:*
>
> *March 1975: Mrs. Dees goes to Atty Holly in Dallas about the delinquency in monies owed from a trust fund set up by her late husband's estate. She tells Holly about the photographs and her desire to sell them. That day she goes to Paris [TX] at Holly's request and brings them back to Holly. Gets receipt.*
>
> *NOTE: The reference to "atty Holly" refers to a Dallas attorney Lamar Holley who had offices in the First Republic Bank building. Holley was Lyndon Johnson's campaign manager in the 1952 Senate race. In 1978, Holley represented Dallas crime boss, Joe Campisi when he appeared before the HSCA.*

> *Chain of custody continued: July 1975 to Jan. 1976 The FBI keeps photographs and turns them over to the Sweiker [sic] Committee.*
>
> *Jan. 1976 Sweiker [sic] Committee turns over photographs to Mrs. Dees. In Dec. 1976*
>
> *Mrs. Dees turned over photographs to the Select Committee on Assassinations. Ricky White turns over his father's rifle stock to Blackmer of the HSCA."*

**Circa 1978**

While living in Paris, Texas, Ricky and Tricia are contacted by Phillip Jordan, a close family friend who informed them that the House Select Committee was going to name Ricky's father as being involved in the Kennedy assassination.

**Circa 1978**

The HSCA issued their final report declaring a high probability that at least two gunmen "*acting independently of one another*" had fired at the President in Dealey Plaza.

**July 10, 1980**

Geneva's mother, Mary Bell Blair died in Paris, Texas, she was 79 years old.

**April 1981**

Ricky and Tricia White moved from Paris, Texas to Midland, Texas.

**October 13, 1982**
Geneva's father, Weldon S. Toland, died at the age of 87 at the McCuistion Medical Center in Paris, Texas.

**October 15, 1982**
Weldon Toland was buried at Hopewell Cemetery in Paris, Texas. After the services, the family returned to the Toland home at 2630 West Houston Street. Onsite, Ricky's cousins found Roscoe's Marine Corps footlocker in a detached shed at the north edge of the property. Inside the trunk, Ricky found his father's military records, letters from home, and assorted military memorabilia. At the bottom of the footlocker, Ricky found his father's diary.

**June 30, 1983**
Geneva divorced Ben K. Dees.

**August 14, 1983**
Geneva married Jerry D. Galle.

**Circa 1986**
Ricky started reading his father's diary for the first time.

**December 3, 1986**
Ricky and Tricia's home in Midland was burglarized; three rifles, a video recorder, a ring, and cash were taken. No suspects were ever identified.

**September 28, 1987**
Ricky and Geneva visited the Oak Cliff branch of Wynnewood State Bank. One of the keys from the bank bag opened safe deposit box #203. Ricky said the box contained $200,000 or $250,000 in Bearer Bonds. A detailed inventory

of the contents was provided by the bank representative. Geneva didn't remember the will had been probated in 1972 and did not inform Ricky. Because of this omission, they were not allowed to claim the contents of the safe deposit box. Ricky remembered his mother telling the bank representative erroneously that her husband's will had not been through the courts. *(See Timeline Entry for December 15, 1972)*

**November 13, 1987**

Ricky, not knowing that the will had already been probated, went to Midland County Assistant District Attorney Al Schorre for assistance. After meeting with Ricky, Schorre agreed to help. (Note: This was the first of three meetings between Ricky and Schorre.) In that initial meeting, Ricky disclosed how he came to possess his father's materials and described some of the items from the footlocker. (Note: Ricky said that he also provided Schorre with the name and location of the bank.)

**December 30, 1987**

Midland County District Attorney's Investigator J.D. Luckie contacted Corporal Jack Beavers of the Dallas Police Intelligence Unit requesting information about former officer Roscoe White. Luckie told Beavers that he was contacted by this man's son, Ricky White, who told him about a safe deposit box containing $200,000 in cash.

**December 31, 1987**

FBI Special Agents Thomas N. Farris, Edward M. Stroz from the El Paso field office and SA John K. Hicks from the Midland field office, initiated mobile surveillance on

Ricky and Tricia White from 7:00 a.m. to 12:40 p.m.

**January 1988**

An undated and unsigned FBI memo from the El Paso field office stating:

> *"White [Ricky] is concerned about his father's death. The father worked for M and M Equipment in Dallas. It was run by Don Rasmussen. The company had a $300,000 insurance policy on White [Roscoe]. Before the father died, Rasmussen had him* [Roscoe] *sign on the policy so it could be placed in trust. Actually, Don and David Rasmussen used the money to their own benefit. The White family got only $40,000."*

Curiously, although the FBI had previously denied any knowledge of a safe deposit box belonging to Roscoe White, the last page of this same memo stated:

> ***"The safety deposit box is Oakcliff [sp] Texas, was actually bought for $3,000 by Roscoe White, Sr. in 1968 and not 1964 as reported."***

A $3,000 price tag for a single safe deposit box was unreasonable. This unheard-of amount caused the authors to think that, at one time, it may have been used by Roscoe White as a **long-term** repository for the materials later found in the canister.

**January 2, 1988**

FBI Special Agents John K. Hicks and Edward M. Storz from the Midland field office continued surveillance on

Ricky and Tricia White. The couple "suspected" that they were being followed, but their suspicions were not confirmed until the release of FBI documents 25 years after the fact.

**January 3, 1988**

SA Thomas N. Farris provided Al Schorre with the address and directions to Ricky and Tricia's home in Midland. (Note: In a phone interview with Ricky's attorney, Bud Fensterwald, Agent Farris denied that he knew Ricky's address.) Schorre and his investigator, J. D. Luckie arrived at Ricky's home around 10:30 a.m. They were allowed to view all of the contents from Roscoe White's footlocker. Later, Schorre provided information to the FBI about this meeting with Ricky.

**January 4, 1988**

Investigator J. D. Luckie contacted FBI Special Agent Kenneth Bersano of the Dallas field office and Corporal Beavers from the Dallas Police Intelligence Unit. According to a SECRET memo prepared by Beavers, Luckie, Beavers, and Bersano claimed that they were unable to locate the bank where the safe deposit box was kept.

**January 12, 1988**

Attorney Jerry Smith from nearby Hereford, Texas, met Ricky and Tricia in their home and examined his father's assassination-related material. Smith spent several hours looking through the material but was not shown the diary. Before leaving, Smith suggested that Ricky make a copy of the diary and allow him to retain a copy for safekeeping.

**January 13, 1988**

FBI Special agents Thomas Farris and Ronald Butler came unannounced to Ricky's home and directed him to pack all his father's assassination-related material into a box, then accompany them to their offices in downtown Midland.

Ricky returned home after a five-hour "interrogation." A short time later, Agent Farris came back to their home claiming that Ricky had accidentally picked up his notebook and that he was there to retrieve it.

**January 14, 1988**

Geneva directed Ricky to bring all his father's material back to her.

**January 20, 1988**

Geneva called Ricky and told him the diary was not in the cardboard box. At that point, Ricky suspected that SA Thomas Farris had taken the diary when he came to his home.

**January 26, 1988**

Investigator J. D. Luckie contacted Dallas Police Intelligence Corporal Jack Beavers and was told that the FBI had now taken over the investigation and that the Midland County DA's office was withdrawing from the case. In Beavers' SECRET memo to his supervisor, he wrote: "*Investigator Luckie said the* ***FBI had met with Ricky White, had seen the pictures and diary*** (emphasis added). In typical FBI fashion, they told Luckie that ".... *there was nothing to what had been alleged by Mr. White."*

**January 28, 1988**
Dallas Police Intelligence Corporal Jack Beavers of the

Dallas Police Intelligence Division submitted the previously discussed SECRET memo about Ricky White.

**August 10, 1988**
Ricky and his friend, Andy Burke, visited the Wynnewood State Bank in Oak Cliff; however, they were denied entry into the safe deposit box vault. They were directed to contact the local FBI office. (Note: This was Ricky's second visit to the bank.)

**November 22, 1988**
A photo taken by Jimmy Rhodes was published in *Time* magazine. The photo showed Jack Ruby looking at an "unidentified woman." Ricky and Tricia identified the "unidentified woman" as Ricky's mother, Geneva White.

**March 7, 1989**
Ricky and Andy Burke visited the Dallas FBI field office and met with Special Agents Paul Shannon and Gary Gerszewski. Ricky and Andy informed the agents that they were writing a book about Ricky's father and his involvement in the Kennedy assassination.

Again, in typical fashion, the FBI refused to seriously consider any and all evidence that pointed to a conspiracy connected to the murder of President Kennedy.

**May 15, 1990**
Ricky scheduled a private meeting with Larry Ray Harris from the JFK Assassination Information Center in Dallas. He told Harris how he discovered his father's military

footlocker and a diary in which his father admitted to his direct involvement in killing President Kennedy. When Harris asked to see the diary; Ricky told him that an FBI agent stole it.

**May 25, 1990**

Larry Ray Harris introduced Ricky and Tricia White to J. Gary Shaw at the JFK Assassination Information Center in Dallas. At that meeting, Ricky admitted that his mother worked for Jack Ruby from September to October 1963, and explained how he discovered his father's diary, in which Roscoe admitted that he shot JFK from the grassy knoll using a 7.65 Mauser. Ricky further explained that his father also confessed, in writing, that he shot and killed Officer Tippit. At this same meeting, Ricky gave Shaw and Harris a metal can containing a 16mm film reel.

**May 29, 1990**

J. Gary Shaw and Texas Certified Legal Investigator Joe West took the film obtained from Ricky to the Kodalux Film Lab in Dallas. The men were told that the only lab capable of developing an Ektachrome movie film was in Aurora, Colorado. (Note: This film stock was stamped "K-II 659650910.")

**May 30, 1990**

J. Gary Shaw, Larry Howard, and Joe West drove to Denver and personally delivered the film to the Rocky Mountain Film Company. After looking at the film, the technician explained that there were no images on the film due to *"age and terrestrial radiation."*

**May 31, 1990**
Larry Howard contacted Kodak corporate headquarters and requested production information for film stock labeled "K-II 659650910." Kodak advised that this stock was first produced in 1961 and was discontinued in 1964.

**June 1, 1990**
Ricky provided a handwritten, notarized affidavit to J. Gary Shaw and witnessed by Joe West and Larry Harris. In the affidavit, Ricky stated that he read in his father's diary where Roscoe described using a 7.65 Mauser to shoot President Kennedy and that he also shot and killed Officer Tippit.

**June 2, 1990 (2 events)**
**1)** Ricky and Joe West visited Wynnewood State Bank in Oak Cliff. (Note: This was Ricky's third trip to the bank.) After several minutes of discussion with the bank employee, the men were allowed into the vault. After handing his key to the bank employee, they were informed that the key did not work.

**2)** Ricky, Joe West and J. Gary Shaw traveled to Paris, Texas to interview Philip Jordan, who refused to let Ricky in the house. Jordan told Ricky that *"Shaw's knowledge of the events is a threat."*

**June 4, 1990**
While examining the assassination material, J. Gary Shaw and Larry Ray Harris found an <u>empty</u> 8mm film container.

**June 6, 1990**
Ricky brought a second roll of film to the JFK Assassination Information Center. Ricky reported that he found the film

inside a small cardboard box among his father's possessions. Attached to the small box was a "sticky note" with the notation, "Military man," in his father's handwriting. Stamped into the perforated end of the film was the film's type and speed identifier, "K II A COLOR 40 ASA K 11."

Before leaving the center, Ricky told Shaw and Harris that his family owned a cabin in the small resort community of Cedar Crest Colony at Lake Whitney, Texas. The property, which had been sold before Roscoe's death, was 80 miles southwest of Dallas. Ricky remembered one day watching his father dig a hole and bury a metal box in the ground. Ricky described the box to be about 12" tall and 7" inches wide. He also remembered reading about this box in his father's diary. (Note: This was not the metal cylinder Ricky found in the attic of his grandparents' home in Paris, Texas.) The "metal box" has never been found.

**June 8, 1990**

Ricky arrived at Gary Shaw's home in Cleburne and met Larry Howard and Joe West. Howard informed Ricky that his mother had been trying to contact him and he needed to call her as soon as possible. The men left Cleburne and traveled to the White's former cabin at Lake Whitney, Texas. Using picks and shovels, the four men dug several large holes around the property but found nothing. Not to be deterred, West arranged for a backhoe to be brought to the property the next day.

**June 9, 1990 (2 events)**

**1)** Ricky, J. Gary Shaw, Larry Howard, and Joe West returned to Lake Whitney and directed the backhoe operator to dig on the northwest side of the cabin. After several hours, the backhoe operator had dug a twelve-foot by twelve-foot

by two-foot-deep hole, but nothing was found. Ricky left Lake Whitney and headed home to Midland, Texas.

**2)** At a truck stop near Eastland, Texas, Ricky called Tricia to inform her of the results of the search at the cabin. Tricia told him that his mother had been trying to reach him all day and that he needed to call her at once. When Ricky called Geneva, she reminded him that his father had helped her father build an addition to the home in Paris, Texas. Geneva suggested that he go there and look in the attic. While driving to Paris, Ricky remembered the small paper sack from his father's footlocker and on the inside of the sack, his father had written a series of Roman numerals and carpenter's notations. Ricky assumed it had something to do with his grandparents' home.

Ricky arrived at his grandparents just after sundown. Ricky entered through an unlocked door at the back of the house, climbed into the attic, and, with the aid of a flashlight, found a metal cylinder covered in a thick coat of dust. This was the first time Ricky had ever seen this item. After removing the canister from the attic, Ricky made several attempts to open the lid, but it was sealed too tightly. When he shook it, he heard something loose moving inside.

Ricky drove the six hours back to Midland and arrived sometime before dawn. Later that day, with Tricia by his side, Ricky had to use a pry bar and strap to loosen the tightly sealed lid.

Inside the canister, Ricky found one of his father's Marine Corps dog tags, a small green textbook on dictation, and 2 sheets of clear plastic. One sheet contained three typed messages, and the other contained family-related photo negatives and newspaper clippings. (Note: Refer to Chapter Six where the green dictation textbook is examined in detail.)

**June 21, 1990**

Larry Ray Harris wrote this memo regarding a private conversation he had with Ricky White:

> *"NOTES OF CONFIDENTIAL CONVERSATION BETWEEN RICKY WHITE AND LARRY RAY HARRIS.*
>
> *Today at 5:00 PM, Ricky Don White came to my residence to brief me on his and Joe West's activities this week in Dallas. He began by telling me that Rev. Jack Shaw had agreed to go to Midland to talk to Geneva and said it was "God's will" that he go to Midland.*
>
> *Then, Ricky said he had something to tell me and he paused for a moment as he struggled with the words. He said Joe [West] was on his way back to Houston and was carrying 'the orders' that his father had received from the Office of Naval Intelligence to kill President Kennedy because he was a threat to national security and world peace.*

> *Ricky told me he had figured out that Roscoe's Roman numerals in the paper sack were carpenter's markings and the word 'Paris' * made Ricky believe it had something to do with his grandmother's house in Paris, Texas. He said this dawned on him while driving back from Lake Whitney. He turned around and drove to Paris and went into the attic of the empty house and looked in the rafters.*
>
> *He found a stainless-steel container with a plunger-type handle and rubber lining. Once he opened the case, he found three typed messages encased in laminate.* *Ricky does not remember telling Larry Harris that the word "Paris" was written on the inside of the sack.

**June 29, 1990**

Kevin Walsh of the Capitol Hill Investigative Agency from Washington, D.C., arrived in Paris, Texas, and interviewed Philip Jordan. The following is a summary of that interview taken directly from Walsh's notes:

> – Jordan is obviously not the man in the Mexico City photograph alleged to have posed as Lee Oswald.
> – Jordan was discharged from the Navy on February 19, 1965. – Says he has known Geneva White since she was fourteen years old but only met Roscoe two times (Note: Ricky knows this to be a lie.).
> – In 1967, Roscoe asked for his help following Geneva's electro-shock therapy.

–Geneva gave him a large, sealed envelope but he did not open it until after Roscoe died.
– He said the envelope contained assassination-related photos and gave it back to Geneva and told her to give it to the FBI.
– Colonel Bond gave Roscoe his orders.
– Jordan said Roscoe asked him to "look out for his son" if anything ever happened to him.
– Jordan tells Walsh he was shot by someone who broke into his house in 1978.
– Jordan believes there was/is a DEA agent with the same name and the suspect believed Jordan was that agent.

**June 29, 1990**

Reverend Jack Shaw interviews Geneva at her home in Odessa, Texas and she provides a written statement where she writes:

– Roscoe knew Jack Ruby before he (Roscoe) joined the police department.
– Ruby had been to their home at least a dozen times and overheard them discussing the assassination plot and that Oswald was being set up as the patsy.
– Six weeks before his death, Roscoe said he *"wanted out"* and told her he was going to be killed.
– She was with Roscoe at a rifle range in Grand Prairie and saw Lee Oswald.
– After she came back from New Orleans, Roscoe confirmed he had killed 10 people.

– Roscoe told her he *"...led 2 lives."*
– Roscoe told her Kennedy had to die because *"...the Bay of Pigs was botched."*
– Officer Tippit was killed because, *"...he wouldn't follow through."*
– Roscoe was given photographs from Marina Oswald and told her to burn the negatives.
– Roscoe knew Beverly Oliver.
– On the day of the assassination, Roscoe left the house in plain clothes and put his police uniform in the car.
– The family owned two cars; she drove a 1957 black Dodge sedan and Roscoe drove a 1962 white Ford Galaxie. (Note: Roscoe mentioned in the diary that he left Dealey Plaza in his white Ford Galaxie, drove to Oak Cliff, and met up with Officer Tippit.)

**July 3, 1990**

Ricky called J. Gary Shaw from Van Horn, Texas, and reported that he had found where his father and other men set up a live firing range. Locating the range triggered a childhood memory for Ricky; he remembered that as a small boy, he had gone to an isolated cabin in the Carrizo Mountains and watched as men shot at mannequins propped up in open-top Jeeps. (Note: During the 1950s, this property was leased to the military by a prominent Van Horn attorney named George Walker. J. Gary Shaw learned that a man with the last name of Bowers leased the property for $3500 during deer season. (Note: A person with the last name of "Bowers" was noted on all three of the cables sent to Roscoe.)

**July 4, 1990**
J. Gary Shaw, Joe West, and Larry Harris met with former CIA operative John Stockwell who was shown copies of the plain-text messages found inside the steel canister. Stockwell's opinion was that the formatting of the messages was *"not out of character in the cables he had seen while he was in the CIA."*

**July 13, 1990**
J. Gary Shaw interviewed Roscoe White's half-brother, Isaac Walton Rogers who told him that the FBI came to him shortly after his brother's death and asked if he had received any books or packages from Roscoe before he died.

**July 14, 1990**
J. Gary Shaw, Larry Ray Harris, Joe West, and Reverend Jack Shaw interviewed Geneva. Geneva's husband, Jerry Galle, was also present during the interview. Geneva identified a photo of Charles Nicoletti as the man whom she met in New Orleans and who threatened her husband's life. This photo was one of eleven unlabeled photos shown to her simultaneously. She recognized photos of Jim Braden, Emilio Santana, and Sam Giancana. She also identified a photo of Johnny Roselli as a man she had seen in the company of her deceased husband.

Geneva commented further that on the day after she returned from New Orleans, she confronted Roscoe, who admitted his role in the assassination of President Kennedy.

**July 20, 1990**
The JFK Assassination Information Center hosted a press

conference about the Roscoe White story in late August. Attorney Bud Fensterwald wrote a letter to J. Gary Shaw and Larry Howard stating:

> *"Just for the record I wish to state that, in my view, delay* [of the press conference] *until Aug 20th is very unwise & very dangerous. Delay can result in one or more deaths, and may screw up the whole detail to boot."*

**July 27, 1990 (2 events)**

**1)** Ricky submitted to a polygraph examination; test results indicated that Ricky answered all questions posed to him truthfully.

**2)** Ricky's attorney, Bud Fensterwald, called the Midland FBI office and spoke to SA Ron Butler who categorically denied that he ever saw or stole Roscoe White's diary. According to Fensterwald's notes, *"Ferris* [sp] *threw up on phone, told Fensterwald to contact SA Butler. No one in FBI saw it – the diary, they do not have it, does not think it exists. Went to every bank in the area, couldn't find the lock box."*

**August 1, 1990**

Larry Howard, his wife, Ricky, and Tricia are flown to Los Angeles to meet with film director Oliver Stone who is preparing to start production on the movie, *JFK.* Stone asked Ricky to bring the green "scrapbook," saying that he may want to use it in his movie. (Note: Ricky initially referred to his father's "scrapbook" as the "Witness Elimination Book."

**August 4, 1990**
On the return flight back from Los Angeles to Dallas, passengers aboard the Delta Airlines flight were told that a bomb threat had been received and they would be making an emergency landing on an isolated runway away from the main terminal.

**August 5, 1990**
An article by Earl Golz was printed in the *Austin American-Statesman* newspaper, entitled, *"Nov. 22, 1963: Another Story Blurs the Facts.*" The article focused on Ricky and his claim that his father was one of President Kennedy's assassins.

**August 6, 1990 (2 events)**
**1)** The JFK Assassination Information Center (JFKAIC) at the West End Marketplace hosted a press conference to announce Ricky's story. Approximately two weeks after the press conference, Ricky and Tricia returned to the JFKAIC. While Ricky met with J. Gary Shaw, Larry Ray Harris, and Bud Fensterwald, Tricia went to an antique store inside the West End Marketplace. While there, a stranger approached her and said, *"Whatever you're involved in, you better get out of it."*

**2)** In an article published in the M*idland Reporter Telegram*, reporter Christopher Elliott interviewed Paul McGaghren, a lieutenant with the Dallas Police Department in 1963 and served on a special police committee that investigated the Kennedy assassination. McGaghren said he first heard stories about Roscoe White's alleged involvement in the assassination six months before the interview. Since that time, he has tried to find anyone who might have known White, but reports, *"No one's ever heard of the guy."*

**August 7, 1990 (3 events)**

**1)** Attorney Bud Fensterwald and J. Gary Shaw met with former Texas Attorney General James Mattox about the allegations made by Ricky White.

**2)** Joe West called FBI Special Agent Thomas Farris and asked for his response to the allegation that he saw and took Roscoe White's diary without Ricky's knowledge. Farris declined to comment and referred West to SA Butler in the El Paso field office.

**3)** Ricky appeared on *Inside Edition* with Bill O'Reilly.

**August 9, 1990**

Ricky appeared on *Larry King Live* in Washington, D.C.

**Circa August 1990**

Ricky and Joe West visited Continental Bank in Oak Cliff (formerly known as Wynnewood State Bank) and requested access to the safe deposit box.

**August 15, 1990**

*Texas Monthly* magazine reporter Gary Cartwright interviewed Ricky for a feature story in the upcoming edition.

**August 16, 1990**

Ricky, his brother Tony, and J. Gary Shaw traveled to Lubbock, Texas where they met with attorney Jerry Smith. The purpose of the meeting was to discuss Smith's initial meeting with Ricky.

**August 29, 1990**

J. Gary Shaw received a phone call from Marina Oswald-Porter, who had read a newspaper article about Roscoe White. She commented that when Roscoe and his family lived at 727 Nottingham in Richardson, she and her daughters were renting a house at 733 Scottsdale, two blocks away. She also mentioned that her daughter, Rachel, attended the same elementary school as Ricky White.

**Fall 1990**

Journalist Bill Klaber interviewed Geneva White at her home in Odessa, Texas. She told Klaber the following:

> – Roscoe arranged for her to work at Jack Ruby's Carousel Club, but she admitted that she did not know why she was hired.
> – Roscoe told her JFK was a security threat and had to be killed.
> – Roscoe admitted he had killed a man in the Philippines and *"had done some stateside."*
> – She overheard Ruby refer to her husband as "Mandarin."
> – After the incident in New Orleans, she flew home and confronted her husband, who confessed to his involvement in the murder of President Kennedy.
> – Roscoe told her he was involved with the Central Intelligence Agency and assumed he was working for the good of his country.

**September 12, 1990**

Geneva appointed Ricky to be her "Special Power of

Attorney" which legally authorized him to enter and take possession of the contents of safe deposit box #203 at the Wynnewood State Bank.

**September 21, 1990**

The headline on the front page of the *Dallas Morning News* read, *"Diary Purportedly Linked to JFK Killing Called a Hoax."* This article and others were syndicated to newspapers across the country reporting that a second diary from Roscoe White had been discovered by his widow. Private investigator Joe West represented this as the "smoking gun" in the assassination. It was quickly determined that this second diary and its contents were a fraud.

**October 30, 1990**

J. Gary Shaw received a call from Gary Cartwright, a respected journalist and staff reporter for *Texas Monthly* magazine advising that he was in "hand-to-hand combat with his boss" over the Roscoe White story. Cartwright told Shaw that his boss believed the Warren Commission but was scared to death of the subject. Cartwright said the Roscoe White story was supposed to be the magazine's cover story but it had been changed by upper management. He said he had to "really fight" to get an eight-page essay on the assassination printed. Cartwright's editor finally agreed to publish the Roscoe White story but it would not be the feature article.

He told Shaw that the Roscoe White story was, *"not what he wished"* and it was *"probably a hoax...but may not be."*

**December 1990**

In the article entitled, *"I Was Mandarin"* published in the December 1990 issue of *Texas Monthly* magazine, author Gary Cartwright discusses Ricky's efforts to determine the validity of his father's involvement in the Kennedy assassination.

In the article, Cartwright wrote: *"Agents of the FBI categorically deny that they saw - much less stole Roscoe White's journal."*

**December 1990**

*Nashua Magazine* (Network Publications), published an article by Woody Woodland entitled *"Ricky Don White."*

**December 19, 1990**

J. Gary Shaw showed Roscoe's "scrapbook" to Gerry Patrick Hemming. He said the book appeared to be a scrapbook similar to those kept secretly by serial murderers. He indicated that prison psychiatrists are familiar with these types of scrapbooks and can make determinations of the state of mind of the man who kept the "scrapbook."

**January 17, 1991**

Assassination eyewitness, Beverly Oliver told British documentary producer Nigel Turner that she saw Roscoe White on the grassy knoll immediately after the shots. According to Beverly, *"He was in uniform but was not wearing a hat or gun belt."*

**January 25, 1991**

Ned Butler, an investigator with the Texas Attorney

General's Office, and Jim Barber, an attorney with Desperado Productions, accompanied Ricky to Wynnewood State Bank. The bank manager was called in, but he did not allow them to access the vault.

However, the manager provided a list of the previous owners of the safety deposit box # 203. All the names on the list had been covered with white-out. After scrapping the white-out from the page, Butler recognized one of the names as someone he knew to be a money launderer. While the three men waited in the bank, the bank manager made 2 or 3 phone calls to someone. After rejoining the three men, he told them he was directed not to allow anyone access to the vault.

**January 26, 1991**

Gary H. Beadel arrived at the JFK Assassination Information Center and told J. Gary Shaw that he had known J. D. Tippit's oldest son, Allen, since the third grade. Beadel provided a sworn affidavit detailing an event at the Tippit home about one month before the assassination. Beadel said he and several boys from the neighborhood were playing at Tippit's house when two men arrived. Allen's father, J.D. Tippit, told the boys to go outside and play – and keep away from the house.

Beadel described one of the men as *"a short dumpy-looking guy"* who wore a black dress hat. The boys called him "John Dillinger" because he looked mean. Beadel looked back at the house several times and saw the "Dillinger" character standing at the front window, staring at them. Beadel saw a picture of Roscoe White in the December issue of *Texas*

*Monthly*; his response was: *"This was the same man who stared at them from the window."*

**February 12, 1991**

Geneva Ruth Toland Galle (White) died at the Odessa Medical Center; she was 49 years old. She was laid to rest in the Field of Honor at Restland Memorial Park, Dallas. However, she was not buried next to her husband, Roscoe White. Reverend Jack Shaw officiated the service. (Note: Two weeks after Geneva died, Ricky and Tricia went to Geneva's house at 4228 Bonham Street in Odessa. While they packed some of Geneva's belongings, the next-door neighbor contacted them. The neighbor explained that on the day Geneva died, she saw two men in suits leaving the house. Later that same day, as the neighbor left her home, she noticed that Geneva's front door was open. The neighbor went in and found Geneva lying on the floor. An ambulance was called, and Geneva was taken to Odessa Medical Center, where she died.)

**March 17, 1991**

Assassination eyewitness Beverly Oliver contacted J. Gary Shaw. She reported that she saw Roscoe White and Dallas Police Sergeant Patrick Dean on the grassy knoll right after the shots were fired at President Kennedy.

**April 2, 1991**

Bud Fensterwald, Washington D.C. attorney, long-time supporter of JFK assassination research, and attorney for Ricky White, died unexpectedly in Alexandria, Virginia; he was 69.

**February 11, 1992**

Ricky received a letter from Dallas Deputy Chief of Police Don Whitten, who wrote:

> *"It has come to my attention you may have copies of material and memorabilia relating to the assassination of President John F. Kennedy, that your father, Roscoe White, acquired while he was an officer for the Dallas Police Department...the Dallas Police Department is*
>
> *conducting a search for any files, records or physical objects pertaining to the assassination."*

**April 16, 1992**

Isaac Walton Rogers, Roscoe's half-brother, was killed in a motorcycle accident; he was 39. (Note: See entry for July 13, 1990.)

**February 13, 1993**

Investigator Joe West died in Houston, Texas; he was 59.

**May 12, 1993**

*The West Texas Connection*, a 12-part investigative report by Becky Neighbors, aired on the Odessa/Midland Texas ABC television affiliate, KMID-TV. This series examined the connection between former Dallas Police Officer Roscoe White and the JFK assassination. (Note: See *"The West Texas Connection"* on YouTube.)

**May 24, 1993**
The final episode of *The West Texas Connection* was broadcast on KMID-TV.

**May 28, 1993**
J. Gary Shaw received a phone call from Ricky; he told Gary that a neighbor came to his place of business and informed him that two white vehicles were parked in front of his (Ricky's) house. The neighbor confronted the men and asked them for identification; one of the men produced FBI credentials. The neighbor told Ricky that a never-before-seen small white pickup he drove up to the cars and stopped.

**June 7, 1993**
Ricky called J. Gary Shaw and told him that two FBI agents came by his place of business in a blue car. Ricky said one of the agents identified himself as "Chris."

**June 8, 1993**
Ricky called J. Gary Shaw again and reported that the FBI came to his workplace; they asked for copies of the *"cables"* and *"green book."*

**June 15, 1993**
Larry Howard, Director of the JFK Assassination Information Center, on directions provided by Ricky, traveled to an isolated cabin in Van Horn, Texas. While there, Howard discovered 2,000 empty shell casings of 6.5mm ammunition in a box inside a small room attached to the cabin. Howard also discovered a large electric generator and a two-way radio system in the cabin.

**January 8, 1994**

JFK Assassination Information Center Co-Founder Larry N. Howard died; he was 53.

**February 21, 1994**

Geneva's second husband, Jerry D. Galle died in Odessa, Texas; he was 55.

**April 19, 1996**

Philip Dale Jordan, a long-time acquaintance of Roscoe and Geneva, died at Veterans Medical Center in Dallas; he was 56.

**April 30, 1993**

In a phone interview broadcast as part of a *West Texas Connection* documentary for KMID-TV, Becky Neighbors told J. Gary Shaw about an "off the record" meeting with J.D. Luckie. In that meeting, Luckie warned her: "*You had better watch your back if you try to see Beavers at DPD. One woman got involved with this and wound up drugged and in a motel. Never taken drugs in her life.*" Luckie also told her that he believed the DA's office was making progress on the case – *"until Schorre turned it over to the FBI."*

**October 5, 1996**

Larry Ray Harris died in an automobile accident; he was 44.

**May 1998**

Ricky and Tricia left Midland, Texas, and moved back to Paris, Texas.

**February 8, 1999**
Roscoe's mother, Lydia "Merle" Harrington-Rogers died; she was 82.

**July 1, 2003**
Assassination researcher Michael Brownloe conducted a video interview with Dallas Police Motor Officer Bobby Hargis, who admitted encountering and speaking to Roscoe White on the grassy knoll immediately after the shots were fired at President Kennedy. Hargis recalled: *"Roscoe White was doing like I was...looking for someone ...he* [Roscoe] *couldn't tell just like I couldn't tell where the shot was coming from."*

**January 19, 2013**
Ricky's older brother, Roscoe Anthony "Tony" White, Jr., died in Lubbock, Texas; he was 53. (Note: Cause of death was listed as suicide.)

**May 16, 2018**
The authors met and interviewed Reverend Jack Shaw at his office in Dallas.

**February 9, 2023**
Geneva's third husband, Ben K. Dees, died in Lubbock, Texas; he was 90.

**July 28, 2023**
Shortly after posting the *Admitted Assassin* book cover on social media, the authors received a phone call from Ricky White; he informed them that his cell phone had been hacked and could not be restored.

**July 30, 2023**

Tricia White told the authors that she received a phone call from a number both she and Ricky recognized. When the call connected, an unknown male said: "Obviously you weren't listening to me when we told you thirty years ago that we start with your first born." Then, the caller disconnected.

# APPENDIX B

## Roscoe Anthony White Military Timeline

**1957**

**February 19, 1957**

Roscoe and Geneva's brother, Benny Toland, arrived at the Navy recruiting station in Dallas and enlisted in the United States Marines. Both signed contracts to serve four years of active duty and two additional years in the Reserves. Roscoe was assigned serial number 1666106 and given a temporary military occupational specialty of 3516, Automotive Mechanic.

**February 22, 1957**

Both recruits reported to the Marine Corp Recruit Depot (MCRD) in San Diego and began twelve weeks of recruit training.

**March 2, 1957**

Roscoe was photographed for the first time as a Marine for his Miscellaneous Information and Index form. This photo was used as his official military identification.

**April 19, 1957**

With a score of 212, Roscoe qualified as a sharpshooter at boot camp with the M-1 Garand .30 caliber rifle.

**May 1, 1957**

Roscoe is promoted to Private First Class (E-1).

**May 18, 1957**

Roscoe graduated boot camp as a member of Platoon 121.

**May 19, 1957**
Roscoe reported to Camp Pendleton, California for basic infantry training. He was assigned to "R" Company, 3rd Battalion, 2nd Infantry Training Regiment.

**July 1, 1957 to July 18, 1957**
Records show that Roscoe was on leave during this time.

**July 26, 1957**
Roscoe was transferred from Camp Pendleton to the Marine Corps Air Station at El Toro, California. This base was the primary base for all fighter squadrons on the west coast and home for the 3rd Marine Air Wing of the 1st Marine Division. When Roscoe arrived at the base, fellow Texan Lee Harvey Oswald had been at the base since July 9, 1967.

(Note: Both men were stationed at El Toro for 31 days.)

**August 21, 1957**
Roscoe left El Toro and arrived in San Diego where he and hundreds of other Marines were put aboard the *USS Bexar*, a Haskell-class attack troop transport. Lee Harvey Oswald was also on the ship.

**August 22, 1957**
The *USS Bexar* departed San Diego. After one week at sea, the *Bexar* stopped in Hawaii and the Marines were given leave.
(Note: Oswald sent a postcard to his mother in Fort Worth while in Honolulu. The card was postmarked August 31, 1957, Honolulu, Hawaii.)

Note: Both men were aboard the *USS Bexar* for 22 days.

**September 12, 1957**

The *USS Bexar* arrived at Yokosuka, Japan, and the soldiers were driven to the Naval Air Station Atsugi. Atsugi was a major United States naval base during the Korean War (1950 to 1953). Note: One of the aircraft based at Atsugi was a CIA U-2 spy plane that flew a high-altitude mission over the Soviet Union on March 1, 1958. (See JFK RIF No. 104-10106-10211).

**September 18, 1957**

Roscoe departed from Yokosuka, Japan, and was taken to the Air Force base at Tachikawa. There he boarded a military aircraft and arrived at Kadena Air Force Base on Okinawa the same day. White was assigned to Marine Observation Squadron 2 (VMO-2), known as the Cherry Deuce. He remained at the base until January 31, 1958.

(Note: Both men were stationed at Atsugi for 5 days.)

(Note: The military base at Tachikawa was used by the CIA as a forward base for operations in East Asia and was the main base for Air America, Southern Air Transport and Civil Air Transport, all front companies of the Agency.)

**November 25, 1957**

Roscoe left Naha, Okinawa aboard the *USS Kemper County (LST-854)* and arrived at Subic Bay, Philippines.

**November 29, 1957**

The *USS Kemper County* docked at Subic Bay, Philippines.

**1958**

**January 7, 1958**

Roscoe takes the General Military Subjects Test (GMST) for consideration for promotion to Corporal.

**January 31, 1958**

Roscoe's service record shows that his primary duty was "Auto Veh Oper." (vehicle operator/driver).

**March 15, 1958**

Roscoe left Subic Bay aboard the *USS Point Defiance (LSD-31)*, a Thomaston-class dock landing ship, and arrived at White Beach, Okinawa.

**March 23, 1958 to August 3, 1958**

Roscoe's service record listed him as being on temporary assigned duty with no assignments.

**May 1, 1958**

Roscoe was promoted to Corporal while serving with MAG-16.

**May 9, 1958**

Roscoe completed a six-week auto mechanics course at Sukiran, Okinawa. He graduated 3rd in his class and was given a new Military Occupational Specialty (MOS), 3516, Automotive Mechanic.

**September 2, 1958**

Roscoe left Japan aboard a military aircraft bound for San Francisco.

**September 3, 1958**
Roscoe arrived from Japan at the Naval Station Treasure Island in San Francisco. After 355 days abroad, his first tour of the Far East was completed.

**October 2, 1958**
Roscoe was assigned to the infantry battalion, "E" Battery, 2nd Battalion, 1st Marine Division, Fleet Marine Force at Camp Pendleton, where he remained until May 10, 1959.

**November 3, 1958**
Lee Oswald left Atsugi, Japan aboard the *USS Barrett* and arrived at the naval base at Treasure Island, San Francisco on November 19.

**December 12, 1958**
Roscoe's second weapons qualification occurred while he was at Camp Pendleton. He qualified with the M-1 Garand with a score of 222 which qualified him as an expert.

**1959**

**January 1, 1959**
Roscoe was promoted to Acting Corporal (E-3).

**February 3-6, 1959**
Roscoe was at Camp Del Mar, Oceanside, California, a military campground and resort associated with Pendleton for use by Marines on active duty and their families.

**February 7, 1959**
Roscoe reported back to the main base at Camp Pendleton.

**May 11, 1959**

Roscoe was assigned to 1st Headquarters Battery, 2nd Battalion, 1st Marine Division.

**May 15, 1959**

Roscoe was promoted to Corporal (E-3).

**July 24, 1959**

Roscoe's third weapons qualification was processed at Camp Pendleton. His overall score was 226, allowing him to retain his rating as an expert.

**December 23, 1959**

Roscoe signed a re-enlistment contract to serve an additional six years.

**December 24, 1959**

While on leave, Roscoe submitted a formal request to attend the Army's artillery school at Fort Sill, Oklahoma.

**December 24, 1959 to January 22, 1960**

Roscoe was listed as being on leave.

**1960**

**February 11, 1960**

Roscoe's military specialty was changed to Basic Fire Control Specialist, (MOS "0800") and he was assigned to the infantry as an artillery specialist.

**February 18, 1960**

Roscoe White was awarded the Good Conduct Medal by the commanding officer of "E" Battery, 2nd Battalion 1st Marine Division, Camp Pendleton.

**May 18, 1960**
Roscoe's MOS was changed to Field Artillery Fire Control Specialist, (MOS "0844").

**June 10, 1960**
Roscoe's fourth weapons qualification occurred at Pendleton. He scored 218, which lowered his rating from expert to sharpshooter.

**July 5, 1960**
Roscoe attended the Army's Artillery and Missile School at Fort Sill, Oklahoma.

**September 13, 1960**
Lee Oswald was granted a hardship discharge from the Marines and received an undesirable discharge, not eligible for reenlistment.

**September 23, 1960**
Roscoe graduated from artillery school.

**September 29, 1960**
Roscoe returned to Camp Pendleton.

**October 1, 1960**
Roscoe was assigned to Headquarters Battery, 2nd Battalion.

**October 4, 1960**
Roscoe's MOS was changed to "0847," (Artillery Meteorological Man).

**December 13, 1960**
Roscoe submitted a formal request for a humanitarian transfer to either a base near Dallas or the base at 29 Palms, California. He wrote, *"This request is due to the illness of my wife...due to her condition, it is not possible for me to take her and the children to my next duty station. This would create almost insurmountable financial problems in view of the necessity of having to employ outside help to care for my children."*

**December 18, 1960 to January 6, 1961**
Roscoe was listed as being on leave during this period.

**<u>1961</u>**

**January 8, 1961**
Roscoe took the General Military Subjects Test (GMST) as part of the process for promotion to Sergeant.

**January 9, 1961**
Roscoe was notified that his humanitarian transfer request did not meet the criteria for a permanent posting to Dallas; however, he was transferred to the Marine base at 29 Palms on a permanent basis.

**February 20, 1961**
Roscoe arrived at 29 Palms and was assigned to Headquarters Battery, 1st Field Artillery Group, Fleet Marine Force. He remained at the base until July 15, 1961.

**February 22, 1961 to March 24, 1961**
Roscoe was listed as being on leave during this period.

**June 16, 1961**
While at 29 Palms, Roscoe scored 227 on his annual weapons qualification which qualified him as an expert.

**July 20 to August 11, 1961**
Roscoe was listed as being on leave during this period.

**September 11, 1961**
Roscoe departed 29 Palms for San Diego and shipped out aboard the *USS General William Mitchell (AP-114)* bound for Okinawa.

**September 27, 1961**
Arrived at the naval air base at Naha, Okinawa, and rejoined Headquarters Battery, 3rd Division.

**October 23, 1961**
Roscoe was notified he failed the General Military Subjects Test (GMST) on the Sergeant's promotion test.

**December 1, 1961**
Roscoe requested the results of the Sergeant's promotion test be waived due to an administrative error.
**December 8, 1961**
Roscoe's request to waive the results of the Sergeant's test was approved.

**December 11, 1961**
While overseas with the Headquarters Battery, 1st Battalion, 12th Marines, Roscoe was promoted to Sergeant (E-5).

<u>**1962**</u>

**January 4, 1962**
Roscoe was granted emergency leave and returned to the United States via military aircraft.

**January 6, 1962 to January 30, 1962**
Roscoe was listed as being on leave during this time.

**February 3, 1962**
Roscoe returned to the Marine base at 29 Palms, California.

**February 5, 1962**
Roscoe left 29 Palms and arrived at Travis Air Force Base in Fairfield, California.

**February 6, 1962**
Departed Travis Air Force Base via military aircraft.

**February 9, 1962**
Arrived at Kadena Air Force Base on Okinawa. <u>Travel records did not indicate the date Roscoe left Kadena Air Force Base or the date he arrived at White Beach, Okinawa.</u>

**March 13, 1962**
Left White Beach, Okinawa aboard *USS Carter Hall (LSD-3)*.

**March 26, 1962 to April 1, 1962**
Arrived on the island of Mindoro, Philippines, and participated in OPERATION TULUNGAN, a war-game exercise in which the U.S. Navy, Marines, the Royal Australian Air Force, and the Philippine military took part.

**April 3, 1962**
Left Mindoro aboard *USS Carter Hall (LSD-3)*.

**April 7, 1962**
Arrived at White Beach, Okinawa.

**May 4, 1962**
Left White Beach, Okinawa aboard *USS Merric (AKA 97)*.

**May 7, 1962**
Arrived at Numazu Beach, Japan.

**July 20, 1962**
On his final weapons qualification at Camp Hansen on Okinawa, Roscoe shot a 220, thereby maintaining his rating as a rifle expert with the M-1.

**September 24, 1962**
Left Iwakuni, Japan aboard military aircraft and arrived at Kadena Air Force Base, Okinawa.

**October 28, 1962**
Left Kadena Air Force Base on Okinawa aboard military aircraft bound for California.

**October 29, 1962**
Arrived at the Marine base at Treasure Island, San Francisco, California.

**November 1, 1962**
A letter dated and submitted by "J.C." (last name illegible on the document) sent a letter endorsing Roscoe's request for a hardship discharge. As of this date, Roscoe had not submitted a formal request for a hardship discharge. The

letterhead on the endorsement shows Perrin Air Force Base in Duncanville, Texas, home of the Air Force's 4780th Air Defense Wing.

(Note: The relationship between Roscoe and the author of this letter was unknown. Apparently, the writer had personal knowledge regarding Geneva's surgery, including where her surgery was performed and her need for post-surgery long-term medical care. Additionally, the letter writer knew that Roscoe had been away from home for extended periods.)

It is unclear how the author knew that Roscoe would request a hardship discharge twelve days before he officially submitted the request to the Commandant of the Marine Corps.

**November 3, 1962 to November 25, 1962**
Records indicated that Roscoe was on leave during this period.

**November 13, 1962**
Roscoe formally requested a hardship discharge from the Marines.

**November 16, 1962**
Roscoe received a Naval Speed Letter from the Commandant of the Marine Corps in Washington, D.C., acknowledging receipt of his request for a hardship discharge.

**December 4, 1962**
There are two certificates recognizing Roscoe's honorable discharge from the Marines; one was dated this date, and the other was February 18, 1963.

**1963**

**November 27, 1963**
Roscoe arrived at the Marine Corps Training Depot at the Naval Air Station in Dallas to await discharge from the Marines.

**December 4, 1963**
Roscoe received a letter from the Commandant of the Marine Corps approving his request for a hardship discharge.

**December 5, 1963**
Roscoe's service records list his status as "Inactive."

**February 18, 1963**
Roscoe Anthony White was honorably discharged from the United States Marines and relieved of his contractual obligation of serving his remaining time in the Reserves.

Roscoe White enlisted in the United States Marines on February 19, 1957, and served five years and ten months (2,190 days) on active duty. During that time, Roscoe took 199 days of leave.

As part of his separation from the military, he was no longer obligated to serve his remaining time in the Reserves and was given an honorable discharge from the Marines.

# APPENDIX C
## Photos and Documents

*Field of Honor, Restland Cemetery, Dallas*

*Geneva dances on table; Commission Exhibit 5304-B*

*Geneva with Ruby*

*Roscoe at hair stylist*

*Roscoe business photo*

*Roscoe wearing a sweater and tie*

*White family photos*
*Top: 1965 Bottom: 1968*

## Ricky White

*Ricky at the Press Conference,*
*JFKAIC, July 1990*

*Ricky at the Press Conference, 1990*

*Ricky holding the canister*

## Roscoe and DPD

*DPD Academy Class #79 Photo*

*Left: Roscoe DPD recruit photo*
*Right: Roscoe Police Academy photo*

*Roscoe - employment photo*

*Officer White ca. 1964-1965*

## United States Marine

*Top photo: Corpl. White and two unidentified Marines; Bottom: Boot Camp Graduation Close-up*

Dress Blues

Fatigues and helmet

*Bottom Left: Acting Cpl., December 18, 1959*
*Bottom Right: On leave, Paris, Texas, 1958*

*Top: Platoon 121, San Diego, 1957*
*Bottom (left): Roscoe and Geneva, San Diego*
*Bottom (right) Pfc White and Geneva, ca.1957*

Top right: Roscoe in a tee-shirt

Above: Roscoe and Lee Oswald, location unknown

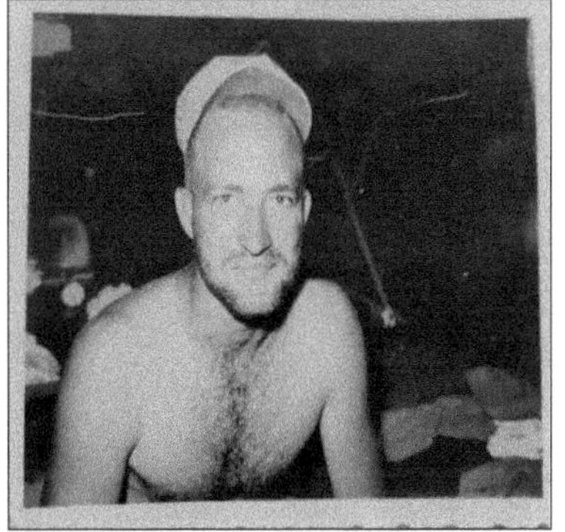

Middle right: Unshaven Roscoe in the field

Left: Roscoe in the field, September 1962

*Roscoe inspects and aims his M-1*

*Roscoe snaps a salute, Paris, Texas, date unknown*

*Roscoe in soft cap, unknown locations*

## The Early Years

*Left: Foreman High School Varsity football offensive line*

*Middle:Roscoe White long snapper*

*Bottom: Varsity football team photo*

*Top: Roscoe in the 7th Grade, 1948*
*Bottom left: Portrait of Geneva Toland, Bottom*
*Right: Roscoe's graduation photo*

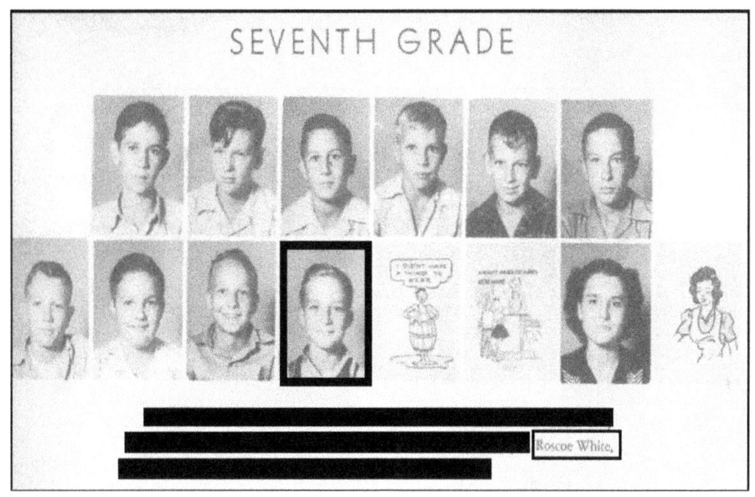

# About the Authors

## J. Gary Shaw

Gary is a retired Texas architect, first-generation researcher, and author who began his investigation of President Kennedy's assassination on November 22, 1963; and he is considered by many as one of the leading authorities on the topic. Additionally, Gary was the co-founder and Vice President of the JFK Assassination Information Center in Dallas and served on the board of directors of the Assassination Archives and Research Center (AARC) in Washington, D.C. From 1990 through 1994, Gary served as the Senior Conference Planner/Moderator for the international "ASK"- JFK assassination symposium in Dallas.

Shaw began to study the assassination in earnest soon after the first books appeared criticizing the findings of the Warren Report. Living in Texas allowed him to conduct hundreds of interviews with those directly connected to the assassination, many of whom were first-hand sources.

In 1976, Shaw, with Larry Ray Harris, wrote and published *Cover-Up: The Governmental Conspiracy to Conceal the Truth About the Public Execution of President Kennedy.* Their work is considered to be one of the more informative early books written on the subject.

Decades before the Internet, Gary spent hundreds of hours interviewing individuals directly connected to the case such as Dallas County Deputy Roger Craig, eyewitness Richard Carr, Beverly Oliver, Karen Carlin, soldiers-of-fortune

Gerry Patrick Hemmings, Roy Hargraves, and others. During his sixty years of research, he has amassed an enormous collection of photographs relating to the assassination and the individuals connected with the crime.

In 1977, Shaw and other distinguished researchers at that time, including Sylvia Meagher, Josiah Thompson, Mark Lane, Larry R. Harris and Mary Ferrell, traveled to Washington, D.C. to confer with the chief counsel and staff of the House Senate Select Committee on Assassinations.

In 1988, Shaw was a consultant and appeared in "Part Three" and in 1995, "Part Six" of Nigel Turner's award-winning British television series documentary, *The Men Who Killed Kennedy*, broadcast on the Arts & Entertainment network. Additionally, Shaw was one of the consultants to Oliver Stone for his movie, *JFK.*

In 1992, Mr. Shaw co-authored the book, JFK*: Conspiracy of Silence* with Dr. Charles Crenshaw and Jens Hansen. Dr. Crenshaw was one of the physicians who attended President Kennedy, Lee Oswald, and Governor John Connally at Parkland Hospital. Furthermore, Dr. Crenshaw was the only Parkland doctor to write a book about his experiences that fateful weekend. The book, *Trauma Room One: The JFK Medical Coverup Exposed,* immediately became a number 1 best-seller on the *New York Times* list of paperbacks. The book was later updated and republished under two different titles, *Trauma Room One* and *JFK Has Been Shot.*

He was a frequent contributor to Penn Jones' *The Continuing Inquiry* and JFKAIC's *Dateline*: *Dallas Publications.*

## Brian K. Edwards

Brian began researching the Kennedy assassination in 1969 and has interviewed numerous individuals directly and indirectly connected to the events of November 22, 1963, including eyewitnesses who were in Dealey Plaza, Dallas police officers, United States Secret Service agents and medical personnel from both Parkland Hospital and Bethesda Medical Center.

From 1978 to 2001, Mr. Edwards served as a police officer with the Lawrence Police Department. During his tenure with the department, he served as a field training officer, accident investigator, police academy, and crime scene photographer. From 1986 to 1996, Brian served with the department's elite Crisis Response Team (CRT).

In 1998, he earned a Master's Degree in Criminal Justice from Washburn University and served as an adjunct instructor in the department until 2005. Mr. Edwards was also an adjunct instructor at several colleges in Kansas, including Ottawa University, Wichita State University, Mid-American University, and Allen County Community College.

Since 1999, Edwards has been a regular presenter at the National JFK Lancer Conference in Dallas, Texas. His research has been cited in numerous publications, including *The Dealey Plaza Echo, Fair Play Magazine, The Kennedy Chronicles, The Fourth Decade, JFK Lancer, Dateline Dallas,* and *Deep Politics Quarterly.*

His original research on the Abraham Zapruder film has been referenced in three scholarly works, including *Assassination Science*; *Murder in Dealey Plaza; The Zapruder Film;* and *The Great Zapruder Film Hoax.*

In 2008, Mr. Edwards co-authored, *Beyond the Fence Line: The Eyewitness Account of Ed Hoffman and the Murder of President Kennedy.*

In 2017, he testified as a witness for the defense in the two-day mock trial of Lee Harvey Oswald at the South Texas College of Law in Houston, Texas.

In 2020, Edwards was a consultant and appeared in Oliver Stone's 4-hour documentary, *JFK Revisited: Through the Looking Glass,* in which he discussed the weapons allegedly used by Lee Oswald.

# Index:

Milton Keynes UK
Ingram Content Group UK Ltd.
UKHW021058170524
442867UK00013B/667